Welcome

To the best and brightest of this beautiful season with *Country Woman Christmas 2003*! Inside, you'll find a celebration of mouth-watering family-favorite recipes, merry craft and gift ideas, do-it-yourself decorating tips and more.

Gathered from *Country Woman* readers across the heartland, each contribution reflects the spirit and down-home traditions of this happy holiday—from cozy farmhouses decked in holly and twinkling lights to rural homesteads echoing with carols and laughter under a starry sky.

We've included inspiring profiles of country women who have found unique ways to bring the holidays home, plus nostalgic stories and poems. And you'll find meal planning for the holidays is a breeze, thanks to the more than 100 never-before-published recipes here.

Hands-on projects from the heart are a part of what we're offering in this keepsake edition, too. It's loaded with fun stocking stuffer ideas, quick-and-easy crafts and lovely handmade items that are sure to become family heirlooms.

All of it comes to you wrapped in wishes for a holiday blessed with family, friends and the promise of peace, goodwill and memories to last a lifetime.

And remember, with a bright new edition added to this series each year, you can look forward to many more country-flavored holiday celebrations ahead.

So no matter how cold it is outside, take time to enjoy the *warmth* of this season...relax and reflect...laugh, light a candle, throw another log on the fire and have yourself a merry country Christmas!

Table of Contents

And Much More!

64

30

79

Executive Editor
Kathy Pohl

Editor
Kathleen Anderson

Food Editor
Janaan Cunningham

Art Director
Emma Acevedo

Associate Editors
Mary C. Hanson
Sharon Selz, Barbara Schuetz

Associate Food Editor
Diane Werner

Senior Recipe Editor
Sue A. Jurack

Recipe Editor
Janet Briggs

Craft Editor
Jane Craig

Art Associate
Tom Hunt

Proofreaders
Jean Steiner, Susan Uphill

Editorial Assistant
Joanne Wied

Test Kitchen Assistant
Rita Krajcir

Food Stylists
Joylyn Jans, Kristin Koepnick

Studio Photographers
Rob Hagen, Dan Roberts

Senior Food Photography Artist
Stephanie Marchese

Photo Studio Manager
Anne Schimmel

Graphic Art Associates
Ellen Lloyd, Catherine Fletcher

Chairman and Founder
Roy Reiman

President
Russell Denson

©2003 Reiman Media Group, Inc.
5400 S. 60th Street
Greendale WI 53129

International Standard Book Number:
0-89821-381-9
International Standard Serial Number:
1093-6750

PICTURED ON OUR COVER. Shown clockwise from lower left: Chocolate Basket with Chocolate-Dipped Fruit (p. 50), wooden Snowman Candy Cane Holder (p. 100), Holiday Truffles (p. 23) and a whimsical Gourd Reindeer and jolly Santa (p. 61).

5

WELCOME To My COUNTRY KITCHEN

By Joan Starkel of Madras, Oregon

I LIKE to think my kitchen is cheery and welcoming all year-round, since our main door opens on that room and it truly *is* the heart of our country home in Madras, Oregon.

But I'm pleased as punch when friends and family "ooh" and "aah" about how *especially* inviting it is at Christmastime.

That's when I pull out all the stops for a merry makeover of the entire room—spicing it up from floor to ceiling with the warm color and aroma of gingerbread!

I start right after Thanksgiving, with husband Robert and daughter Megan, 15, eager to help haul out the holly and boxes of gingerbread trinkets and trims.

Beginning at the top, we wreathe the room in garlands strung with chunky little gingerbread boys, bunches of sweet-smelling cinnamon sticks, big brown ginger cookies and homespun fabric hearts.

(Because of those hearts, I'm good to go until Valentine's Day, so it's always late February before I have to pack away the decorations we love so much!)

Next, I spruce up our view of Oregon's Ochoco Mountains by replacing our everyday window curtains with festive rounded valances brightened with gingerbread boys and girls. I crafted the toppers myself using a little ingenuity and some pre-stamped tree skirts I cut in half!

Wreaths hanging in each window are fashioned from bow-tied evergreens and still more gingerbread boys.

Three in One

It all started 20 years ago, when Robert and I gutted three small rooms to make our "dream kitchen" in the farmhouse that used to belong to his parents. We wanted a space that was open, easy to work in and accessible.

Because Robert is a building supply manager and very talented, we were able to do all the work ourselves—from designing and crafting the dark wood cabinets to building a handy stovetop island in the center of the room to putting in the countertops and breakfast bar.

We also painted the dark wood-paneled walls a soft off-white with accents of peach and blue-gray, and replaced the old carpet with a vinyl floor, made to look like tile, in matching neutral shades.

Choosing New Hues

But I soon found that traditional red Christmas trims clashed with my new countertops in burnt-orange (I call it "cinnamon" today!) and my peachy accents.

So I decided on warm sugar-and-spice gingerbread tones to wrap up our kitchen for the holidays. Since then, my collection of all things gingerbread has grown with the years…and my delicious theme has worn just as well as our original kitchen design.

Our handy breakfast bar—decked out in a gingerbread-boy runner, place mats, napkins and puffy seat cushions—is always ready for holiday visitors. I like to sew and quilt when not working as a school secretary, so it was no trouble whip-

GINGERBREAD GALORE adds sugar and spice to the Oregon kitchen of Joan Starkel (upper left). One festive figure (inset at far right) holds Joan's collection of fabric ginger-boy ornaments made with her mother and sister years ago.

Photos: Dean Guernsey/Central Oregon Images

GOOD ENOUGH TO EAT describes Joan's cozy kitchen during the holidays. Lighted ceramic gingerbread houses and gumdrop trees (left) fill one corner...gingerbread also trims curtains, candles, countertops and cook.

ping up that batch of gingerbread trims myself.

The breakfast bar is the first place company stops to sit, chat or have a cup of coffee. It's also where we eat every day. So we add candles scented with cinnamon, ginger and nutmeg and dinnerware sprinkled with hearts and more ginger-kids when I'm serving up hot cider and holiday fare.

Crop of Collectibles

Raising cattle and alfalfa on our working mini farm of 40 acres raises plenty of dust and dirt in the process! And since our kitchen door is the only one anyone ever uses, even our vinyl floors—chosen for their easy cleaning—boast bright gingerbread rugs at Yule time.

Family and friends tell me that since I've become a collector, they always know what to get me for Christmas. And birthdays. And any and all special occasions...

So now, gingerbread cookie cutters in all sizes trim our kitchen walls, along with shaped platters and pans. Stuffed sets of boy and girl gingerbread dolls sit on windowsills and straddle shelves.

A collection of lighted ceramic gingerbread houses is displayed on a corner table covered with snowy batting and sprinkled with gumdrop trees.

Gingerbread towels brighten the sink, gingerbread magnets decorate the fridge...and gingerbread hot pads and apron cover the cook! This year, I even found a wonderful gingerbread cookie jar to add to my collection.

Most precious to me of all these things, however, is a big resin gingerbread boy that holds a collection of raggedy old gingerbread ornaments my sister and I made from fabric scraps when we were kids. Mom would help us cut and stitch them and hang them on our tree. Once I bring that fellow out, it's Christmas!

It's funny the way things work out sometimes. What began as a decor dilemma is now a tradition for adding sugar and spice and everything nice to our holiday season. Maybe it's even sent some decorating tips your way—along with the merriest of Christmas wishes from our country kitchen to yours!

Photos: Jeff Baird

Holiday Spirit Flavors the Fruits of This Baker's Labor

FRUITCAKE was never Dottie Turner's favorite holiday food. "I could pretty much take it or leave it," she recalls from her home in Brattleboro, Vermont.

But the holiday *tradition* of fruitcake was something this founder of Gram's Fruitcake Company didn't want to give up.

"My aunt and uncle had a lovely ritual of making fruitcake together on the day after Thanksgiving to give to the whole family," Dottie explains. "They did it for decades—until it got to be too much for them."

At that point, Dottie and husband Phil decided to keep the tradition going. The weekend after Thanks-

giving in 1964, the couple gathered their ingredients, the largest mixing bowl they could find and began their own 2-day ritual of baking fruitcakes.

"We started by using a recipe we found in a magazine. It called for a little fruit and a lot of citron. We sent it out to family, but nobody loved it," she remembers. "The next year, we made our own citron, thinking it would taste better. It didn't."

It was when they cut out the citron altogether and experimented with different dried fruits that they began getting rave reviews from their family and friends.

"Imagine a fruitcake without all those little colored pieces," describes Dottie. "Ours has no citron, no candied fruits, no artificial ingredients, no artificially prepared *anything.*

"We use only dried fruits, many organically grown—raisins, dates, apricots, pineapple, figs, cranberries and currants. Plus, we add fresh almonds and walnuts and lots of brown sugar and cinnamon."

Each cake is aged until it resembles a steamed pudding—very dense, moist, dark and rich. "Most people say they never knew fruitcake could taste like ours. Even our five young grandsons choose it over other snacks," Dottie chuckles.

Four years ago, at the urging of friends and family, Dottie decided to make her fruitcake available over the Internet…and created Gram's Fruitcake Company. The number of repeat customers has grown ever since.

Dottie does all the cutting, mixing, baking, wrapping and packing herself. Last year, she single-handedly turned out more than 200 pounds of fruitcake from her home kitchen—and hopes to double that amount this Christmas.

Obviously, her cherished family tradition has become a tasty tradition for other families, too!

Editor's Note: For details, write to Gram's Fruitcake Company, Box 2296, W. Brattleboro VT 05303 or visit *www.gramsfruitcake.com.* ✳

FRUITS OF THE SEASON, along with brown sugar, cinnamon and a treasured family tradition, are all part of the success of Gram's Fruitcakes. Busy Vermont baker Dottie Turner (top) bakes, wraps and sells her fruitcakes all year long, turning out more than 200 tasty pounds last year.

Eggs-acting Artist Creates Holiday Collectibles

SOME PEOPLE might be unnerved by a job that calls for skills as diverse as delicately decorating eggshells one day—and driving a tractor or building a fence the next!

But not Sylvia Satterwhite Smith. She's too busy keeping up with the demand for her intricately painted eggs, then helping husband Bob work their Tahlequah, Oklahoma ranch.

"We raise cattle and Quarter Horses, board horses for other people and bale hay for them and us," says Sylvia, who married Bob 15 years ago. "We're making up for a late start with a lot of hard work."

Both are retired from Northeastern State University, where they met and where the idea for Sylvia's home-based business was hatched in 1985. Asked to think of "a souvenir" the school could sell during its annual 2-week Christmas fest, she tried painting eggshell ornaments. "And every single egg sold out the first night!" she recalls.

Today, customers from Germany, Japan, Australia, Canada, Denmark, Peru, Holland, Hawaii and all over the U.S. collect Sylvia's eggs—including many men who buy her wildlife work.

"But my Christmas eggs sell 10 to one over other subjects, so I paint them year-round," she says. "I select eggs to fit the design I'm painting—fat round eggs for fat round subjects like wreaths or Santas. Long slim eggs are better for trees, candles or the Holy Family."

She collects eggs from hatcheries, farms and friends and turns them into works of art in the studio Bob built for her over their garage.

"I use eggs of all sizes—from nickel-sized quail eggs to duck, goose, emu and ostrich eggs the size of honeydew melons," she notes.

"I usually sketch my design first with pencil, trace over it in ink, erase the pencil lines and begin painting directly on the egg. I use acrylic paint like watercolors, layering it to achieve the look I want.

"Once an egg is completely painted, I dip it in an acrylic coating six to ten times, letting it dry thoroughly each time. That helps to preserve it.

"I decorate up to 50 eggs at once, painting all the red areas on every egg, then all the green, etc. It's a time-consuming art."

And one that has definitely touched the hearts of many egg enthusiasts. "It's a God-given talent I'm happy to share with others," Sylvia says with a smile.

Editor's Note: *For more details on Sylvia's eggs, contact her by mail at Satterwhite's Sundown Studio, 21048 E. 810 Road, Tahlequah OK 74464.* ❋

CARTONS OF KEEPSAKES. Sylvia Satterwhite Smith (top) stays busy year-round hatching new designs for her delicately painted Christmas eggshell ornaments.

Grandma's Brag Page

SEASON'S REASON. Grandkids Matthew and his baby sister Hannah are already learning the Christmas story, writes Cora Austin of Manor, Pennsylvania.

SANTA'S FAVORITE DEERE? Makes sense to little Ellie Slick, who can't think of a better way to haul out the holly. "She comes by it naturally," writes Grandma Marge Wayne, "since that's the only kind of machinery we ever use on our farm in Yorkville, Illinois."

TWICE-BLEST is how Great-Grandma Ola Maude Wilson feels about twins Ricky and Destiny Wilson. "Having these little darlings at our place in Sturgis, Mississippi for the holidays is sure to make the season bright," she writes. "They are our pride and joy."

LITTLEST ANGEL Sarah Kaitlen is a "miracle", says Grandma Jeanine Fairbank from Destin, Florida, who snapped her heaven-sent cherub.

WHERE'S MR. CLAU*ZZZ*? Little 4-month-old Luke tried to keep his eyes open on Christmas morning, but Grandma Claudette Arsenault of Summerside, Prince Edward Island (and Mickey!) caught him falling asleep.

LITTLE SHAVERS. Grandsons Kevan and Bryan Smith put on Santa caps, shaving cream beards and holiday smiles as doting Grandma Nancy Chandler of Cicero, New York snapped away.

Bountiful Brunch

Perfect for a holiday brunch, these festive recipes are guaranteed to warm hearts, widen eyes, fill tummies and light up Christmas morning!

CREAMY STRAWBERRY CREPES
Kathy Kochiss, Huntington, Connecticut
(Pictured on page 12)

As special as Christmas morning itself, these delicate crepes add a merry touch of elegance and holiday color to brunch!

    4 eggs
    1 cup milk
    1 cup cold water
    2 tablespoons butter *or* margarine, melted
1/4 teaspoon salt
    2 cups all-purpose flour
Additional butter *or* margarine
FILLING:
    1 package (8 ounces) cream cheese, softened
1-1/4 cups confectioners' sugar
    1 tablespoon lemon juice
    1 teaspoon grated lemon peel
1/2 teaspoon vanilla extract
    4 cups fresh strawberries, sliced, *divided*
    1 cup whipping cream, whipped

In a mixing bowl, beat eggs, milk, water, butter and salt. Add flour; beat until smooth. Cover and refrigerate for 1 hour. In an 8-in. nonstick skillet, melt 1 teaspoon butter; pour 2 tablespoons of batter into the center of skillet. Lift and tilt pan to evenly coat bottom. Cook until top appears dry; turn and cook 15-20 seconds longer. Remove to a wire rack. Repeat with remaining batter, adding butter to skillet as needed. When cool, stack crepes with waxed paper or paper towels in between.

For filling, in a small mixing bowl, beat the cream cheese, confectioners' sugar, lemon juice, peel and vanilla until smooth. Fold in 2 cups of berries and the whipped cream. Spoon about 1/3 cup filling down the center of 15 crepes; roll up. Garnish with remaining berries. Freeze remaining crepes for another use. **Yield:** 15 filled crepes.

EGG BRUNCH BAKE
Iva Combs, Medford, Oregon
(Pictured on page 12)

Here's a great way to serve ham and eggs to a crowd—and it's so easy to prepare. Best of all, everyone's eggs will be hot and ready at the same time with this savory, satisfying dish.

    2 tablespoons butter *or* margarine, melted
    2 cups (8 ounces) shredded cheddar cheese
    2 cups cubed fully cooked ham
12 eggs
    1 can (5 ounces) evaporated milk
    2 teaspoons prepared mustard
Salt and pepper to taste

Drizzle butter into a greased shallow 3-qt. baking dish. Sprinkle with cheese and ham. In a mixing bowl, combine the eggs, milk, mustard, salt and pepper; beat well. Pour over ham and cheese. Bake, uncovered, at 350° for 40-45 minutes or until a knife inserted near the center comes out clean. Let stand for 5-10 minutes before serving. **Yield:** 6-8 servings.

JOLLY JELLY DOUGHNUTS
Lee Bremson, Kansas City, Missouri
(Pictured on page 12)

Just looking at these fat, festive, jelly-filled doughnuts will make your mouth water. Serve warm and you'll find folks licking sugar from their fingers and asking for seconds.

    2 packages (1/4 ounce each) active dry yeast
    2 cups warm milk (110° to 115°)
    7 cups all-purpose flour, *divided*
    4 egg yolks
    1 egg
1/2 cup sugar
    1 teaspoon salt
    2 teaspoons grated lemon peel
1/2 teaspoon vanilla extract
1/2 cup butter *or* margarine, melted
Oil for deep-fat frying
Red jelly of your choice
Additional sugar

In a large mixing bowl, dissolve yeast in warm milk. Add 2 cups flour; mix well. Let stand in a warm place for 30 minutes. Add the egg yolks, egg, sugar, salt, lemon peel and vanilla; mix well. Beat in butter and remaining flour. Do not knead. Cover and let rise in a warm place until doubled, about 45 minutes.

Punch dough down. On a lightly floured surface, roll out to 1/2-in. thickness. Cut with a 2-1/2-in. biscuit cutter. Place on lightly greased baking sheets. Cover and let rise until nearly doubled, about 35 minutes.

In a deep-fat fryer or electric skillet, heat oil to 375°. Fry doughnuts, a few at a time, for 1-1/2 to 2 minutes on each side or until browned. Drain on paper towels. Cool for 2-3 minutes; cut a small slit with a sharp knife on one side of each doughnut. Using a pastry bag with a small round tip or a small spoon, fill each doughnut with about 1 teaspoon jelly. Carefully roll doughnuts in sugar. Serve warm. **Yield:** about 2-1/2 dozen.

● Hosting a holiday brunch this year? Take a lesson from St. Nick. Detailed shopping and menu lists—made ahead of time and checked twice—are key to getting organized and staying within your budget. And a timeline can keep you cool, on schedule—and the event merry!

JINGLE-BELL BRUNCH. Pictured from top to bottom (p. 12) are these breakfast bell-ringers: Jolly Jelly Doughnuts, a hearty Egg Brunch Bake and festive Creamy Strawberry Crepes.

CHEESY SAUSAGE STROMBOLI
Barbara Lindsey, Manvel, Texas

One taste of this yummy sausage loaf at a Christmas party years ago, and I knew I'd be taking the recipe home for the holidays. A hit back then, it's become a family tradition. I like to serve it with hash brown potatoes and a fruit salad.

     2 pounds bulk pork sausage
     1 medium onion, chopped
 1/2 cup shredded Colby-Monterey Jack cheese
 1/2 cup grated Parmesan cheese
     2 eggs, beaten
     2 tablespoons minced fresh parsley
 1/2 teaspoon salt
 1/2 teaspoon hot pepper sauce
     1 package (16 ounces) hot roll mix
     1 tablespoon butter *or* margarine, melted
Picante sauce

In a skillet, cook sausage and onion over medium heat until meat is no longer pink; drain. Transfer to a bowl. Stir in the cheeses, eggs, parsley, salt and hot pepper sauce; cool.

   Prepare hot roll mix according to package directions. Roll dough into a 17-in. x 14-in. rectangle. Spoon filling over dough to within 1 in. of edges. Roll up jelly-roll style, starting with a long side. Seal seams and tuck ends under. Place seam side down on a greased baking sheet. Bake at 400° for 20-25 minutes or until golden brown. Brush with butter. Let stand for 10 minutes before slicing. Serve with picante sauce. **Yield:** 8-10 servings.

APPLE CHEDDAR MUFFINS
Brenda Hildebrandt, Moosomin, Saskatchewan

If you like tart apples and cheese, you'll love these moist, merry muffins. My family insists I make them for the holidays, but they're so easy to fix that I often whip up a batch or two on camping and canoe trips as well.

     2 cups all-purpose flour
 1/3 cup sugar
     1 teaspoon baking powder
 1/2 teaspoon baking soda
 1/4 teaspoon salt
 1/4 teaspoon ground cinnamon
1-1/2 cups (6 ounces) shredded cheddar cheese,
        divided
 1/3 cup grated Parmesan cheese
     1 egg
     1 cup buttermilk
 1/4 cup vegetable oil
     2 medium tart apples, peeled and chopped

In a large bowl, combine the first six ingredients; stir in 1 cup cheddar cheese and Parmesan cheese. In a small bowl, beat the egg, buttermilk and oil; stir into dry ingredients just until moistened. Fold in apples.

   Fill greased or paper-lined muffin cups three-fourths full. Sprinkle with the remaining cheddar cheese. Bake at 400° for 20-22 minutes or until a toothpick comes out clean. Cool for 10 minutes before removing from pan to a wire rack. **Yield:** 1 dozen.

HERBED SAUSAGE GRAVY OVER CHEESE BISCUITS
Lynn Crosby, Homerville, Ohio

The gang at my house loves anything with biscuits, and this oregano-flavored sausage gravy is the best we've ever tasted! It's a real favorite with my husband and two toddlers.

     2 cups all-purpose flour
     3 teaspoons baking powder
 1/2 teaspoon salt
 1/2 cup milk
 1/4 cup vegetable oil
     2 teaspoons dried oregano
 1/2 pound bulk mozzarella cheese, cut into 8 cubes
GRAVY:
 1/2 pound bulk pork sausage
 3/4 cup milk
     1 teaspoon dried oregano
 1/4 cup all-purpose flour
     1 cup cold water

In a large bowl, combine the flour, baking powder and salt. Stir in milk and oil just until moistened. Turn onto a lightly floured surface. Roll to 1/2-in. thickness; cut with a floured 2-1/2-in. biscuit cutter. Place a pinch of oregano in the center of each biscuit; top with a cheese cube. Moisten edge of dough with water and pull up over cheese, forming a pouch; pinch tightly to seal. Place on a lightly greased baking sheet. Bake at 450° for 12-15 minutes or until golden brown.

   Meanwhile, in a skillet, cook the sausage over medium heat until no longer pink; drain. Stir in the milk and oregano. Combine the flour and water until smooth; add to sausage mixture. Bring to a boil; cook and stir for 2 minutes or until thickened. For each serving, spoon about 1/3 cup gravy over two biscuits. **Yield:** 4 servings.

CORNY POTATO FRITTATA
David Heppner, Brandon, Florida

Here's a zesty skillet frittata that's fast, flavorful and easy to fix. It's sure to give your breakfast crowd a hearty, stick-to-the-ribs jump start on busy holiday mornings.

     6 green onions, sliced
     2 garlic cloves, minced
     2 tablespoons vegetable oil
     1 large potato, peeled and cut into 1/4-inch cubes
     2 cups frozen corn, thawed
     6 eggs
     1 cup (4 ounces) shredded mozzarella cheese
 1/2 teaspoon salt
 1/4 teaspoon pepper

In a 10-in. ovenproof skillet, cook onions and garlic in oil for 2 minutes. Add potato; cook and stir over low heat for 10 minutes. Add corn; cook and stir for 2 minutes.

   In a bowl, beat eggs. Stir in the cheese, salt and pepper. Pour over potato mixture. Cover and cook for 6 minutes or until eggs are nearly set. Meanwhile, preheat broiler. Uncover skillet and place 6 in. from the heat for 2-3 minutes or until eggs are completely set. Cut into wedges. **Yield:** 4-6 servings.

AMBROSIA COMPOTE
Marilou Robinson, Portland, Oregon
(Pictured at right)

This sparkling fruit salad is versatile and pretty enough for dessert. I like to vary the fruits…and will sometimes top them off with a dollop of ginger-laced whipped cream or Yuletide star fruit garnish.

      1 can (20 ounces) pineapple chunks
      3 medium firm bananas
      1 cup seedless red grapes
      3 medium navel oranges, peeled and sectioned
      1 cup flaked coconut, *divided*
      1/2 cup ginger ale, chilled
Sliced star fruit, optional

Drain pineapple, reserving juice in a large bowl. Slice bananas into the bowl; toss to coat. Add the pineapple, grapes, oranges and half of the coconut; toss to coat. Cover and refrigerate for up to 4 hours.

   Just before serving, pour ginger ale over salad and sprinkle with remaining coconut. Serve with a slotted spoon. Garnish with star fruit if desired. **Yield:** 6-8 servings.

COFFEE PUNCH
Diane Propst, Denver, North Carolina

Guests will sing your praises when you ladle out this frothy, frosty, ice cream-coffee punch. Try brewing it with different flavored coffees for a perky pick-me-up.

      1 quart brewed vanilla-flavored coffee, cooled
      1 can (12 ounces) evaporated milk
      1/2 cup sugar
      1/2 gallon vanilla ice cream, softened
Ground cinnamon

In a large container, combine the coffee, milk and sugar; stir until sugar is dissolved. Spoon ice cream into a punch bowl; pour coffee mixture over the top. Sprinkle with cinnamon. Serve immediately. **Yield:** 2-1/2 quarts.

HOLIDAY BURRITOS
Antoinette Metzgar, Rio Rancho, New Mexico

In the Southwest, a breakfast burrito wraps up potatoes, eggs and cheese with a unique "Feliz Navidad" ("Merry Christmas") flair! There are many variations, but this is our favorite and it always wins compliments from guests.

      1/4 cup chopped onion
      1/2 cup butter *or* margarine
      2 pounds red potatoes, cut into 1/2-inch cubes
      12 eggs, lightly beaten
      1 teaspoon garlic salt
      1 teaspoon salt
      1/2 teaspoon pepper
      2 to 3 cans (4 ounces *each*) chopped green
         chilies, drained
      12 flour tortillas (8 inches), warmed
      2 cups (8 ounces) shredded cheddar cheese

In a large skillet, saute the onion in butter until tender. Add the potatoes; cover and cook for 15-20 minutes or until tender. In a bowl, combine the eggs, garlic salt, salt and pepper; pour over potatoes. Cook and stir over medium heat until the eggs are completely set. Stir in the chilies. Fill each tortilla with about 3/4 cup of the egg mixture and 2 heaping tablespoons of the cheese; roll up tightly. Serve immediately. **Yield:** 12 burritos.

FRENCH TOAST WITH SPICED BUTTER
Mabel Brown, Elmira, Ontario

My whole family arrives early on Christmas morning—all of them looking for this delicious French toast with its cinnamon and nutmeg butter. It's easy to make and serve—and always a hit! Children enjoy it as much as my adult guests.

      4 eggs
      1 cup milk
      2 tablespoons sugar
      1/2 teaspoon vanilla extract
      6 slices French bread (3/4 inch thick)
      2 tablespoons butter (no substitutes)
SPICED BUTTER:
      1/2 cup butter, softened
      1/4 cup confectioners' sugar
      1/2 teaspoon ground cinnamon
      1/4 teaspoon ground nutmeg
Maple syrup

In a bowl, beat eggs. Whisk in the milk, sugar and vanilla. Arrange bread in a greased 11-in. x 7-in. x 2-in. baking dish; pour egg mixture over top. Turn to coat. Cover and refrigerate overnight.

   In a skillet, melt butter over medium heat. Add bread; cook for 3-4 minutes on each side or until golden brown. Meanwhile, in a small mixing bowl, cream the butter, confectioners' sugar, cinnamon and nutmeg. Serve French toast with spiced butter and syrup. **Yield:** 3 servings.

Holiday Breads

HOME-BAKED HOLIDAY BREADS. Clockwise from top right: Old-World Dark Bread (p. 18), Jalapeno Cornmeal Muffins (p. 19), Spiced Walnut Scones (p. 18), Herbed Mozzarella Round (p. 19) and Orange-Hazelnut Breakfast Twists (p. 18).

There's nothing like the aroma of bread baking to warm heart and home. Served fresh from the oven or given as gifts, homemade breads bring a taste of the holidays!

SPICED WALNUT SCONES
Kim Lueras, Eureka, California
(Pictured on page 17)

Yuletide visitors might stop by just for a taste of these moist and tender scones! Chock-full of walnuts and drizzled with orange-peel glaze, they are wonderful with a cup of coffee.

    3/4 cup milk
      2 tablespoons lemon juice
      3 cups all-purpose flour
    3/4 cup sugar
      1 tablespoon grated orange peel
      1 teaspoon baking soda
      1 teaspoon ground nutmeg
    1/2 teaspoon baking powder
    1/8 teaspoon ground cloves
    1/8 teaspoon ground mace
    1/2 cup cold butter (no substitutes)
    1/2 cup chopped walnuts
GLAZE:
      1 cup confectioners' sugar
      3 to 4 teaspoons orange juice
    1/2 teaspoon grated orange peel
    1/4 teaspoon almond extract

In a bowl, combine milk and lemon juice; let stand for 2 minutes. In a large bowl, combine the flour, sugar, orange peel, baking soda, nutmeg, baking powder, cloves and mace; cut in butter until mixture resembles coarse crumbs. Add walnuts and milk mixture; stir just until moistened.

Turn onto a floured surface; knead 10 times. Divide dough in half. Roll each portion into a 7-in. circle; cut each into six wedges. Separate wedges and place 1 in. apart on greased baking sheets. Bake at 400° for 18-20 minutes or until golden brown. Remove to wire racks. Combine glaze ingredients until smooth; drizzle over warm scones. **Yield:** 1 dozen.

ORANGE-HAZELNUT BREAKFAST TWISTS
Loraine Meyer, Bend, Oregon
(Pictured on page 16)

These buttery spirals won a Blue Ribbon at Oregon's State Fair. Friends always ask for more when I bring these to church gatherings. They add a merry note to Christmas morning!

3-3/4 to 4 cups all-purpose flour
      1 cup mashed potato flakes
    1/4 cup sugar
      2 packages (1/4 ounce *each*) quick-rise yeast
      2 teaspoons grated orange peel
      1 teaspoon salt
      1 cup milk
    1/2 cup butter *or* margarine
    1/2 cup sour cream
    1/4 cup water
      2 eggs

FILLING:
    1/2 cup confectioners' sugar
    1/4 cup butter *or* margarine, softened
      1 cup ground hazelnuts *or* walnuts
ORANGE GLAZE:
    1/4 cup sugar
    1/4 cup orange juice
      2 tablespoons butter *or* margarine
    1/4 cup sour cream

In a large mixing bowl, combine 3 cups flour, potato flakes, sugar, yeast, orange peel and salt. In a saucepan, heat milk, butter, sour cream and water to 120°-130°. Add to dry ingredients; beat just until blended. Beat in eggs until smooth. Stir in enough remaining flour to form a soft dough. Turn onto a lightly floured surface; knead until smooth and elastic, about 3 minutes. Place in a greased bowl, turning once to grease top. Cover and let rise until doubled, about 25 minutes.

Meanwhile, for filling, combine confectioners' sugar and butter in a bowl. Stir in hazelnuts. For glaze, in a saucepan, bring sugar, orange juice and butter to a boil. Boil for 3 minutes. Remove from the heat; let stand for 10 minutes. Stir in sour cream; set aside.

Punch dough down; turn onto a lightly floured surface. With a long side facing you, roll into a 22-in. x 12-in. rectangle. Spread filling over bottom half of dough. Fold dough over filling; seal edges. Cut into 22 strips, 1 in. each. Twist each strip 4-5 times. Shape strips into a circle and pinch ends to seal. Place in greased 15-in. x 10-in. x 1-in. baking pans. Cover and let rise until doubled, about 25 minutes. Bake at 375° for 15-20 minutes or until golden brown. Cool for 5 minutes before removing from pans to wire racks. Immediately drizzle with glaze. **Yield:** 22 rolls.

OLD-WORLD DARK BREAD
Irina Baker, Avondale, Arizona
(Pictured on page 17)

I came up with this recipe in an attempt to re-create a wonderful Russian bread I enjoyed as a child. It makes a dense, crusty loaf that dark-bread lovers are sure to savor.

      4 to 4-1/2 cups all-purpose flour
      4 cups rye flour
      2 cups All-Bran
      2 packages (1/4 ounce *each*) active dry yeast
      2 tablespoons instant coffee granules
      1 tablespoon sugar
      1 tablespoon salt
      1 tablespoon caraway seeds
      1 teaspoon fennel seed, crushed
    1/2 teaspoon ground coriander
      3 cups water, *divided*
    1/2 cup molasses
    1/4 cup butter *or* margarine, cubed
      2 tablespoons cider vinegar
      1 square (1 ounce) unsweetened chocolate
      1 tablespoon cornstarch

In a large mixing bowl, combine the first 10 ingredients. In a saucepan, heat 2-1/2 cups water, molasses, butter, vinegar and chocolate to 120°-130°. Add to dry ingredients; beat just until moistened. Turn onto a floured surface; knead until smooth and elastic, about 6-8 minutes. Place in a greased bowl, turning once to grease top. Cover and let rise in a warm place until doubled, about 1-1/2 hours.

Punch dough down. Turn onto a lightly floured surface. Divide dough in half; shape each portion into a ball. Place on greased baking sheets. Cover and let rise until doubled, about 30 minutes. Bake at 375° for 50-55 minutes or until golden brown. Remove from pans to wire racks to cool. In a small saucepan, combine the cornstarch and remaining water until smooth. Bring to a boil; cook and stir for 1-2 minutes or until thickened. Brush over bread. **Yield:** 2 loaves.

JALAPENO CORNMEAL MUFFINS
Molly Schultz, Hatley, Wisconsin
(Pictured on page 17)

My husband and I love anything spicy hot, but these zippy jalapeno-studded muffins also add color to our holiday table. Serve them with chili to warm up your caroling party!

```
    2 tablespoons plus 3/4 cup cornmeal, divided
1-1/4 cups all-purpose flour
    2 tablespoons sugar
    3 teaspoons baking powder
    1 teaspoon salt
    1/4 teaspoon cayenne pepper
    2 eggs, lightly beaten
    1 cup milk
    1/4 cup butter or margarine, melted
    4 jalapeno peppers, seeded and chopped*
```

Grease 12 muffin cups and sprinkle with 2 tablespoons cornmeal; set aside. In a bowl, combine the flour, sugar, baking powder, salt, cayenne and remaining cornmeal. Combine the eggs, milk and butter; stir into dry ingredients just until moistened. Fold in jalapenos.

Fill prepared muffin cups two-thirds full. Bake at 400° for 20-25 minutes or until a toothpick comes out clean. Cool for 5 minutes before removing from pan to a wire rack. Serve warm. **Yield:** 1 dozen.

*Editor's Note: When cutting or seeding hot peppers, use rubber or plastic gloves to protect your hands. Avoid touching your face.

HERBED MOZZARELLA ROUND
June Brown, Veneta, Oregon
(Pictured on page 16)

Served warm with soup or salad, this pretty bread is hearty enough to round out a quick meal during busy holidays.

```
4-1/4 to 4-3/4 cups all-purpose flour
    2 packages (1/4 ounce each) active dry yeast
    1 tablespoon sugar
    1 teaspoon salt
    1 cup warm mashed potatoes (prepared with milk
      and butter)
```

```
    1/2 cup butter or margarine, softened
    1 cup warm milk (120° to 130°)
    3 cups (12 ounces) shredded mozzarella cheese
    1 to 3 teaspoons minced fresh thyme
    1 teaspoon minced fresh rosemary
TOPPING:
    1 egg
    1 tablespoon milk
    1 teaspoon poppy seeds
```

In a large mixing bowl, combine 3 cups flour, yeast, sugar and salt. Add potatoes and butter. Beat in warm milk until smooth. Stir in enough remaining flour to form a firm dough. Beat for 2 minutes. Turn onto a lightly floured surface; knead until smooth and elastic, about 5-7 minutes. Place dough in a greased bowl, turning once to grease top. Cover and let rise in a warm place until doubled, about 45 minutes.

Punch dough down; turn onto a lightly floured surface. Roll into an 18-in. circle. Transfer to a lightly greased 14-in. pizza pan. Sprinkle cheese over center of dough to within 5 in. of edge. Sprinkle with thyme and rosemary. Bring edges of dough to center; twist to form a knot. Cover and let rise until doubled, about 30 minutes.

In a small bowl, combine egg and milk; brush over top. Sprinkle with poppy seeds. Bake at 350° for 40-45 minutes or until golden brown. Cool for 20 minutes before slicing. Serve warm. **Yield:** 1 loaf.

HERB ROLLS
Julie Dykstra, Canyon Country, California

Because they start with convenient refrigerated biscuits, these buttery "homemade" treats couldn't be easier to make.

```
    1/4 cup butter or margarine, melted
    1 tablespoon grated Parmesan cheese
    1/4 teaspoon dried minced onion
    1/2 teaspoon garlic powder
    1/2 teaspoon dried parsley flakes
    1/2 teaspoon dill weed
    1 tube (12 ounces) refrigerated buttermilk
      biscuits
```

In a bowl, combine the butter, Parmesan cheese, onion, garlic powder, parsley and dill. Spread in a 9-in. pie plate. Cut biscuits into quarters; place in plate and turn to evenly coat with herb mixture. Arrange biscuit pieces in a single layer. Bake at 400° for 10-12 minutes or until golden brown. **Yield:** 8-10 servings.

● Quick breads (also muffins, scones and biscuits) are made with baking powder or baking soda instead of yeast. They are ready to bake in minutes during busy holidays and make great gifts. Here are some quick tips for quick breads:

Do not overmix, as this will toughen the texture.

Do not overbake. Check doneness 10-15 minutes early.

Do not eat too soon! Breads made with zucchini, bananas or cranberries slice and taste best a day after baking.

GERMAN STOLLEN
Christin Dupee, Chesterfield, Virginia

I traditionally bake three of these flavorful favorites just before Thanksgiving to enjoy on Christmas and New Year's, too.

8-1/2 to 9 cups all-purpose flour
    1 cup plus 2 tablespoons sugar, *divided*
    2 packages (1/4 ounce *each*) active dry yeast
    2 teaspoons salt
    2 cups milk
1-3/4 cups butter *or* margarine, softened, *divided*
    4 eggs
1-1/2 teaspoons almond extract
    1 teaspoon grated lemon peel
    1 teaspoon rum extract, optional
1-1/2 cups slivered almonds
    1 cup *each* chopped candied cherries, candied
        lemon peel and candied orange peel
    1 cup raisins
GLAZE:
    1 cup confectioners' sugar
    1/4 teaspoon vanilla extract
    2 to 3 tablespoons milk

In a large mixing bowl, combine 3 cups flour, 1 cup sugar, yeast and salt. In a saucepan, heat the milk and 1-1/2 cups butter to 120°-130°. Add to dry ingredients; beat just until moistened. Beat in eggs until smooth. Stir in enough remaining flour to form a soft dough. Add the almond extract, lemon peel and rum extract if desired. Stir in the almonds, cherries, candied lemon and orange peel and raisins (dough will be slightly sticky).

Turn onto a heavily floured surface; knead until smooth and elastic, about 6-8 minutes. Place in a greased bowl, turning once to grease top. Cover and let rise in a warm place until almost doubled, about 1-1/2 hours.

Punch dough down; turn onto a lightly floured surface. Divide into thirds. Roll each portion into a 15-in. x 8-in. oval. Melt remaining butter. Brush each oval with 1 tablespoon butter and sprinkle with 2 teaspoons of the remaining sugar. Fold a long side of oval to within 1/2 in. of the opposite side; press edges lightly to seal. Place on parchment-lined or lightly greased baking sheets. Curve ends slightly. Cover and let rise for 30 minutes.

Bake at 350° for 30-35 minutes or until golden brown. Brush with remaining melted butter; remove from pans to wire racks to cool. Combine the glaze ingredients; drizzle over stollen. **Yield:** 3 loaves.

SOUR CREAM CRESCENTS
Judie Anglen, Riverton, Wyoming

My family insists I make these dinner rolls to complement our holiday feasts. They can be made ahead and frozen.

    3 teaspoons active dry yeast
    1/3 cup warm water (110° to 115°)
    1/2 cup sugar
    1/2 teaspoon salt
    1 cup butter (no substitutes), softened
    1 cup (8 ounces) sour cream
    2 eggs
    4 cups all-purpose flour

In a large mixing bowl, dissolve yeast in warm water. Beat in the sugar, salt, butter, sour cream and eggs until smooth. Add 3 cups flour; mix well. Stir in the remaining flour. Cover and refrigerate for 6 hours or overnight.

Punch dough down; turn onto a floured surface. Divide into four pieces. Roll each portion into a 10-in. circle; cut each into 12 wedges. Roll up wedges from the wide end; place pointed side down 3 in. apart on greased baking sheets. Curve ends down to form crescent shape. Cover and let rise in a warm place until doubled, about 1-1/2 hours. Bake at 375° for 15 minutes or until golden brown. Remove from pans to wire racks. **Yield:** 4 dozen.

MOLASSES HERB CASSEROLE BREAD
Sandi Pichon, Slidell, Louisiana

A friend of my mother's gave her the recipe for this crusty round loaf that I now bake for my family. It goes great with winter stews and soups…and we love the hint of molasses.

3-1/3 to 3-2/3 cups all-purpose flour
    1 package (1/4 ounce) active dry yeast
    1 teaspoon salt
    1/2 teaspoon dried oregano
1-1/4 cups milk
    1/4 cup molasses
    2 tablespoons butter *or* margarine
    1 tablespoon dried minced onion
    1 egg

In a large mixing bowl, combine 2 cups flour, yeast, salt and oregano. In a saucepan, heat the milk, molasses, butter and onion to 120°-130°. Add to dry ingredients; beat until combined. Beat in egg until smooth. Stir in enough remaining flour to form a firm dough. Beat on high speed for 3 minutes. Turn onto a floured surface; knead until smooth and elastic, about 5-7 minutes. Place in a greased bowl, turning once to grease top. Cover and let rise in a warm place until doubled, about 1 hour.

Punch dough down. Place in a greased 2-qt. round baking dish. Cover and let rise until doubled, about 40 minutes. Bake at 350° for 40-45 minutes or until browned. Remove from pan to a wire rack to cool. **Yield:** 1 loaf.

APPLE COFFEE CAKE PIZZA
Dorothy Schaller, Bruce, South Dakota

This family favorite has a delicious fresh apple-pie taste that brightens any holiday table or brunch. I've made it for years.

2-1/2 to 3 cups all-purpose flour
    2 tablespoons sugar
    1 package (1/4 ounce) active dry yeast
    3/4 teaspoon salt
    1/3 cup water
    1/3 cup milk
    3 tablespoons butter *or* margarine
    1 egg
CHEESE TOPPING:
    2 packages (3 ounces *each*) cream cheese,
        softened
    3 tablespoons sugar

1/2 teaspoon ground cinnamon
APPLE TOPPING:
   1/2 cup sugar
     2 tablespoons all-purpose flour
     1 teaspoon ground cinnamon
     5 medium apples, peeled and chopped
   1/4 cup butter *or* margarine, cubed
STREUSEL:
   1/2 cup all-purpose flour
   1/2 cup sugar
   1/2 cup old-fashioned oats
   1/2 cup butter *or* margarine, softened
     1 tablespoon ground cinnamon
GLAZE:
     2 cups confectioners' sugar
     2 tablespoons lemon juice

In a large mixing bowl, combine 1-1/2 cups flour, sugar, yeast and salt. In a saucepan, heat the water, milk and butter to 120°-130°. Add to dry ingredients; beat just until moistened. Beat in egg until smooth. Stir in enough remaining flour to form a soft dough. Turn onto a floured surface; knead until smooth and elastic, about 6-8 minutes. Place in a greased bowl, turning once to grease top. Cover and let rise in a warm place until doubled, about 1 hour.

Punch dough down. Press into two greased 12-in. pizza pans; build up edges. In a small mixing bowl, combine the cheese topping ingredients. Spread over dough to within 1/2 in. of edges. In a saucepan, combine the apple topping ingredients; simmer, uncovered, until apples are tender. Spoon over cream cheese layer.

Combine streusel ingredients; sprinkle over apples. Let stand for 15 minutes. Bake at 375° for 30-35 minutes or until crust is browned. Combine glaze ingredients; drizzle over warm pizzas. Cool on wire racks. **Yield:** 2 coffee cake pizzas (6-8 servings each).

BANANA NUT BREAD
Dita Franklin, San Diego, California

Even Santa wouldn't guess grated potatoes are the "secret ingredient" that makes this quick bread so delightfully moist.

   1/2 cup butter *or* margarine, softened
1-1/2 cups sugar
     2 eggs
     3 medium ripe bananas, mashed
   1/3 cup buttermilk
     4 cups all-purpose flour
     1 teaspoon baking powder
     1 teaspoon baking soda
     1 teaspoon salt
1-1/2 cups grated peeled uncooked potatoes
     1 cup chopped walnuts

In a mixing bowl, cream butter and sugar. Add eggs; mix well. Combine bananas and buttermilk. Combine flour, baking powder, baking soda and salt; add to creamed mixture alternately with banana mixture. Stir in potatoes and walnuts. Transfer to two greased 9-in. x 5-in. x 3-in. loaf pans. Bake at 350° for 45-55 minutes or until a toothpick inserted near center comes out clean. Cool for 10 minutes before removing from pans to wire racks. **Yield:** 2 loaves.

LEMON-TWIST LOAVES
Audrey Thibodeau, Mesa, Arizona
(Pictured above)

Christmas at our house just wouldn't be the same without this mouth-watering tangy twist with its pretty glaze.

     2 cups water
     3 cups sugar, *divided*
     1 cup butter *or* margarine, *divided*
     2 packages (1/4 ounce *each*) active dry yeast
   3/4 teaspoon salt
     1 egg
     1 egg yolk
     7 cups all-purpose flour
     1 cup sliced almonds, chopped
     3 tablespoons grated lemon peel
GLAZE (optional):
     3 cups confectioners' sugar
     3 tablespoons grated lemon peel
     3 to 4 tablespoons milk
     1 teaspoon lemon extract
     1 cup sliced almonds, toasted

In a saucepan, bring water and 1 cup sugar to a boil. Remove from heat; add 1/2 cup butter. Cool to 110°-115°; transfer to a mixing bowl. Beat in yeast, salt, egg and egg yolk. Add 4 cups flour; beat until smooth. Stir in enough remaining flour to form a soft dough. Turn onto a floured surface; knead until smooth and elastic. Place in a greased bowl, turning once to grease top. Refrigerate for 8 hours.

Punch dough down; divide into thirds. On a floured surface, roll each portion into a 16-in. x 10-in. rectangle. Melt remaining butter; spread over dough. Combine the chopped almonds, lemon peel and remaining sugar; sprinkle over butter. Roll up jelly-roll style, starting with a long side; press edges and ends to seal.

Place on greased baking sheets. With a knife, cut loaves in half lengthwise to within 1 in. of one end. Holding the uncut end, loosely twist strips together. Cover and let rise until doubled, about 2 hours. Bake at 350° for 25-30 minutes. Combine first four glaze ingredients; spread over warm bread. Sprinkle with toasted almonds. **Yield:** 3 loaves.

Goodies for Gifts

'Tis the season for fun and flavorful gifts from the kitchen. Wrap up these merry snack fixin's, cookie mixin's, spreads and breads to delight drop-in guests or busy hostesses.

CHRISTMAS COOKIES IN A JAR
Lori Daniels, Beverly, West Virginia
(Pictured on page 22)

With layers of vanilla chips, oats and dried cranberries, this delectable cookie mix looks as good as it tastes! For a special gift, tuck jar in a pretty basket with wooden spoon, cookie sheet, kitchen timer and instructions.

  1/3 cup sugar
  1/3 cup packed brown sugar
  3/4 cup all-purpose flour
  1/2 teaspoon baking powder
  1/8 teaspoon baking soda
  1/8 teaspoon salt
    1 cup quick-cooking oats
    1 cup orange-flavored dried cranberries
  1/2 cup vanilla *or* white chips
ADDITIONAL INGREDIENTS:
  1/2 cup butter *or* margarine, melted
    1 egg
    1 teaspoon vanilla extract

In a 1-qt. glass jar, layer the sugar and brown sugar, packing well between each layer. Combine the flour, baking powder, baking soda and salt; spoon into jar. Top with oats, cranberries and chips. Cover and store in a cool dry place for up to 6 months.

To prepare cookies: Pour cookie mix into a large mixing bowl; stir to combine. Beat in butter, egg and vanilla. Cover and refrigerate for 30 minutes. Drop by tablespoonfuls 2 in. apart onto ungreased baking sheets. Bake at 375° for 8-10 minutes or until browned. Remove to wire racks to cool. **Yield:** 3 dozen.

HOLIDAY TRUFFLES
Jennifer Lipp, Bucharest, Romania
(Pictured on page 22)

I like to lavish the chocolate lovers on my list with these sumptuous truffles. They always bring me rave reviews.

    3 packages (12 ounces *each*) semisweet chocolate
      chips, *divided*
2-1/4 cups sweetened condensed milk, *divided*
  1/2 teaspoon orange extract
  1/2 teaspoon peppermint extract
  1/2 teaspoon almond extract
1-1/2 pounds white candy coating, melted
  3/4 pound dark chocolate candy coating, melted
  1/2 cup ground almonds

In a microwave-safe bowl, melt one package of chips. Add 3/4 cup milk; mix well. Stir in orange extract. Repeat twice, adding peppermint extract to one portion and almond extract to the other. Cover and chill for 45 minutes or until firm enough to shape into 1-in. balls. Place on three separate waxed paper-lined baking sheets. Chill for 1-2 hours or until firm.

Dip the orange-flavored truffles twice in white candy coating; place on waxed paper to harden. Dip peppermint-flavored truffles in dark chocolate coating. Dip almond-flavored truffles in dark chocolate, then roll in ground almonds. If desired, drizzle white coating over peppermint truffles and dark chocolate coating over orange truffles. **Yield:** about 7 dozen.

BRAIDED SESAME WREATH
Debbie Sadlo, Landover, Maryland
(Pictured on page 22)

"Knead" a gift better than store-bought? This is the all-time favorite bread of everyone I know—and I bake all kinds. I garnish my buttery braided wreaths with festive fabric bows.

    1 package (1/4 ounce) active dry yeast
    1 cup plus 2 tablespoons warm milk
      (110° to 115°)
  1/4 cup butter *or* margarine, melted
  1/4 cup sugar
    1 egg
    1 teaspoon salt
    4 to 4-1/4 cups all-purpose flour
TOPPING:
    1 egg, beaten
    1 teaspoon sesame seeds

In a large mixing bowl, dissolve yeast in warm milk. Add the butter, sugar, egg, salt and 2 cups flour; beat until smooth. Stir in enough remaining flour to form a soft dough. Turn onto a floured surface; knead until smooth and elastic, about 6-8 minutes. Place in a greased bowl, turning once to grease top. Cover and let rise in a warm place until doubled, about 1 hour.

Punch dough down. Turn onto a lightly floured surface; divide into thirds. Shape each portion into a 22-in. rope. Place ropes on a greased baking sheet and braid; pinch ends together to form a ring. Cover and let rise until doubled, about 45 minutes. Brush with egg and sprinkle with sesame seeds. Bake at 350° for 20-25 minutes or until golden brown. Remove from pan to a wire rack to cool. **Yield:** 1 loaf.

● Wrapping make-ahead gift goodies is easy if you save empty Christmas card boxes, says Darlene Smith of Rockford, Illinois. Just cover the handy personal-size cookie and candy containers with foil, fill with treats and freeze. Later, thaw and add bright bows to the boxes.

GIFTS IN GOOD TASTE. Everyone on your list is sure to enjoy Christmas Cookies in a Jar (and on plate), Holiday Truffles and Braided Sesame Wreath (p. 22, clockwise from top right).

LIME MINT JELLY
Gloria Jarrett, Loveland, Ohio

You're sure to spread Christmas cheer with gift jars of this holly-green jelly that won me a "Best of Show" at the county fair. Flavored with lime, it's delicious on roasted meats.

    4 cups sugar
1-3/4 cups water
    3/4 cup lime juice
      7 drops green food coloring, optional
      1 pouch (3 ounces) liquid fruit pectin
      3 tablespoons finely chopped fresh mint leaves
    1/4 cup grated lime peel

In a large saucepan, combine the sugar, water and lime juice; add food coloring if desired. Bring to a boil over high heat, stirring constantly. Add the pectin, mint and lime peel; bring to a full rolling boil. Boil for 1 minute, stirring constantly.

    Remove from the heat; skim off foam. Pour hot mixture into hot sterilized jars, leaving 1/4-in. headspace. Adjust caps. Process for 15 minutes in a boiling-water bath. **Yield:** 5 half-pints.

ELEPHANT EARS
Susan Taul, Birmingham, Alabama

They'll remember these crispy home-baked pastries long after they've licked the last bit of cinnamon-sugar off their fingers! Great with hot coffee, these make a super gift.

1/2 cup warm milk (110° to 115°)
1/4 cup warm water (110° to 115°)
    1 package (1/4 ounce) active dry yeast
    2 cups all-purpose flour
4-1/2 teaspoons sugar
1/2 teaspoon salt
1/2 cup cold butter (no substitutes)
    1 egg yolk, beaten
FILLING/TOPPING:
    6 tablespoons butter, melted, *divided*
    2 cups sugar
3-1/2 teaspoons ground cinnamon
1/2 cup finely chopped pecans

In a bowl, combine the milk, water and yeast; set aside. In a large mixing bowl, combine the flour, sugar and salt. Cut in butter until mixture resembles coarse crumbs. Add egg to yeast mixture; beat into dry ingredients until blended. Cover and refrigerate for at least 2 hours.

    Punch dough down; turn onto a lightly floured surface. Knead several times. Cover and let rest for 10 minutes. Roll into an 18-in. x 10-in. rectangle. Brush with 2 tablespoons butter. Combine sugar and cinnamon; sprinkle 1 cup over dough. Beginning with a long side, roll up jelly-roll style; pinch edges to seal. Cut into 1-in. slices.

    For each elephant ear, sprinkle a small amount of the remaining cinnamon-sugar on a piece of waxed paper. Place a slice of dough on cinnamon-sugar; roll into a 5-in. circle. Place sugared side down on an ungreased baking sheet. Brush with some of the remaining butter; sprinkle with pecans and cinnamon-sugar. Bake at 375° for 9-11 minutes or until golden brown. **Yield:** 1-1/2 dozen.

CINNAMON POPCORN
Katheryne Ann Johnson, Vernon, Texas

Seasoned with cinnamon, this popcorn is the perfect family snack to munch while watching those classic Christmas movies together.

    4 quarts popped popcorn
    1 cup butter *or* margarine
2/3 cup sugar
    1 tablespoon cinnamon

Place popcorn in a large bowl. In a microwave-safe bowl, combine the butter, sugar and cinnamon. Microwave on high for 1 minute; stir. Microwave 1 minute longer or until the butter is melted. Pour over popcorn and toss to coat. Transfer to two greased 15-in. x 10-in. x 1-in. baking pans. Bake, uncovered, at 300° for 10 minutes. Cool. Store in an airtight container. **Yield:** 4 quarts.

APRICOT-NUT WHITE FUDGE
Betty Claycomb, Alverton, Pennsylvania

My family looks forward to this luscious apricot-studded fudge every year. It's easy to make and really does melt in your mouth. I like to wrap up small squares of the candy with ribbon and silk holly.

    1 package (8 ounces) cream cheese, softened
    4 cups confectioners' sugar
  12 squares (1 ounce *each*) white baking chocolate, melted and cooled
1-1/2 teaspoons vanilla extract
    3/4 cup chopped walnuts *or* pecans
    3/4 cup chopped dried apricots

Line a 9-in. square pan with aluminum foil. Coat with nonstick cooking spray; set aside. In a large mixing bowl, beat cream cheese until fluffy. Gradually beat in confectioners' sugar. Gradually add the white chocolate. Beat in vanilla. Fold in nuts and apricots. Spread into prepared pan. Cover and refrigerate for 8 hours or overnight. Using foil, lift fudge from pan; cut into squares. **Yield:** about 2-1/2 pounds.

CREOLE SEASONING
Jan Buchanan, Ventura, Iowa

This spicy seasoning adds warmth—in more ways than one!—to the holidays and all year-round. The versatile mix is as good on popcorn as it is on chicken or potato wedges. Try packaging it in pretty shakers.

2/3 cup cayenne pepper
1/2 cup plus 2 teaspoons salt
1/4 cup garlic powder
1/4 cup onion powder
1/4 cup chili powder
    2 tablespoons plus 2 teaspoons pepper

In a bowl, combine all ingredients. Store in an airtight container for up to 6 months. **Yield:** about 2 cups.

ORANGE COCONUT CREAMS
Julie Fornshell, Bismarck, North Dakota

Originally a gift from our neighbors, this recipe has become one of our own favorites to make and give at the holidays.

        1 can (14 ounces) sweetened condensed milk
    1/2 cup butter (no substitutes), cubed
        1 package (2 pounds) confectioners' sugar
        1 cup flaked coconut
1-1/2 teaspoons orange extract
        2 cups (12 ounces) semisweet chocolate chips
        2 packages (4 ounces *each*) German sweet
            chocolate
        2 tablespoons shortening

In a saucepan, combine the milk and butter. Cook and stir over low heat until the butter is melted. Place the confectioners' sugar in a mixing bowl. Add milk mixture; beat until smooth. Add the coconut and orange extract; mix well. Roll into 1-in. balls; place on waxed paper-lined baking sheets. Refrigerate until firm, about 1 hour.

   In a saucepan, combine the chips, chocolate and shortening. Cook and stir over low heat until smooth. Dip balls into chocolate. Place on waxed paper until set. **Yield:** 9 dozen.

JERKY PARTY MIX
Lisa Coffell, Swartz Creek, Michigan

Talk about a popular gift! Our friends get such a kick out of this spicy twist on an old party-mix favorite, they ask for it at Christmas, New Year's and even the Fourth of July.

        4 cups *each* Corn Chex, Rice Chex and Wheat
            Chex
        2 packages (3 ounces *each*) Beer Nuts
    1/2 cup butter *or* margarine, melted
        1 envelope taco seasoning
        1 package (4 ounces) beef jerky, cut into bite-size
            pieces

In a large bowl, combine cereal and nuts. In a small bowl, combine butter and taco seasoning; mix well. Pour over cereal mixture and toss to evenly coat. Transfer to two greased 15-in. x 10-in. x 1-in. baking pans. Bake, uncovered, at 250° for 1 hour, stirring every 15 minutes. Stir in beef jerky. Cool completely, stirring several times. **Yield:** about 13 cups.

SNAPPY HORSERADISH DILL PICKLES
Sharon Keech, Madelia, Minnesota

These pickles are a great last-minute gift because they are so easy to make—a little horseradish adds zip to a jar of purchased pickles. They're in hot demand at Christmas! My husband and three grown sons can't get enough of them.

        1 jar (32 ounces) whole dill pickles
    1/3 cup prepared horseradish
    3/4 cup sugar
    1/2 cup water
    1/2 cup cider vinegar

Drain and discard juice from pickles. Slice pickles into spears and return to jar. Add horseradish. In a saucepan, bring the sugar, water and vinegar to a boil. Remove from the heat; cool slightly. Pour over pickles. Cool completely. Cover jar and shake. Refrigerate for at least 8 hours or overnight. **Yield:** 1 quart.

EGGNOG FRUIT BREAD
Margo Stich, Rochester, Minnesota
(Pictured below)

Presents from the pantry are a tradition in my family—and this moist, fruity quick bread is a favorite. I wrap loaves in cellophane and garnish with stickers and curly ribbons.

        3 eggs
        1 cup vegetable oil
1-1/2 cups sugar
    3/4 teaspoon vanilla extract
    3/4 teaspoon rum extract
1-1/2 cups eggnog*
        3 cups all-purpose flour, *divided*
        2 teaspoons baking powder
    1/2 teaspoon salt
    1/2 teaspoon ground nutmeg
        1 cup candied fruit
    1/2 cup chopped walnuts

In a mixing bowl, beat the eggs and oil. Add the sugar, extracts and eggnog; mix well. Combine 2-1/2 cups flour, baking powder, salt and nutmeg; gradually add to egg mixture. Toss the fruit with remaining flour; stir into batter. Fold in walnuts. Pour into two greased 8-in. x 4-in. x 2-in. loaf pans. Bake at 350° for 60-65 minutes or until a toothpick comes out clean. Cool for 10 minutes before removing from pans to wire racks. **Yield:** 2 loaves.

   *Editor's Note: This recipe was tested with commercially prepared eggnog.

Yuletide Sweets

Treat your family and friends to a sleighful of mouth-watering Christmas confections and snacks that are sure to satisfy even Santa's sweet tooth.

SESAME TOFFEE
Janet Owen, Kalamazoo, Michigan
(Pictured on page 26)

I make more cakes and cookies than candy, but I love to stir up a batch of this toffee for Christmas because it's so easy!

  2 teaspoons plus 3/4 cup butter (no substitutes), softened, *divided*
1/3 cup light corn syrup
2/3 cup sugar
1/2 cup sesame seeds, toasted

Line a 15-in. x 10-in. x 1-in. baking pan with foil and grease the foil with nonstick cooking spray; set aside. Grease the sides of a large heavy saucepan with 2 teaspoons butter. Add the corn syrup and remaining butter; cook over medium heat until butter is melted.

Add sugar and sesame seeds; cook and stir until mixture comes to a boil. Cook and stir until mixture turns golden brown and a candy thermometer reads 300° (hard-crack stage). Pour into prepared pan (do not scrape sides of saucepan). Spread evenly. Cool; break into pieces. **Yield:** about 3/4 pound.

WALNUT CARAMEL TREATS
Machelle Wall, Rosamond, California
(Pictured on page 26)

Better than visions of sugarplums, these triple-decker treats feature creamy caramel and nuts sandwiched between milk chocolate layers—a candy lover's dream come true!

  2 teaspoons plus 1/3 cup butter (no substitutes), *divided*
  2 packages (11-1/2 ounces *each*) milk chocolate chips, *divided*
  4 tablespoons shortening, *divided*
  2 packages (14 ounces *each*) caramels*
1/4 cup water
  3 cups chopped walnuts

Line an ungreased 9-in. square pan with foil and grease the foil with 2 teaspoons butter; set aside. In a microwave or heavy saucepan, melt one package of chips and 2 tablespoons shortening; stir until smooth. Pour into prepared pan. Refrigerate for 20 minutes.

Meanwhile, in a heavy saucepan over medium-low heat, combine the caramels, water and remaining butter. Cook and stir until caramels are melted and mixture is smooth. Stir in walnuts. Pour over chocolate layer. Refrigerate for 45 minutes.

In a microwave or heavy saucepan, melt remaining chips and shortening. Spread over caramel layer. Cover and re-frigerate for at least 2 hours or until firm. Using foil, lift candy out of pan. Discard foil; cut candy into squares. Store in the refrigerator. **Yield:** about 4 pounds.

  *Editor's Note: Recipe tested with Hershey's caramels.

CANDY CANE POPCORN BALLS
Rebecca Gove, Cape Neddick, Maine
(Pictured on page 26)

When I was a little girl, my mother and I made these popcorn balls for family and friends at Christmas. Now my husband and I carry on the tradition, turning out more than 250 each December—and still our list keeps growing!

  4 quarts popped popcorn
  2 teaspoons water
  1 teaspoon baking soda
1/2 teaspoon vanilla extract
  1 cup light corn syrup
1/4 cup butter (no substitutes)
  2 cups sugar
 24 miniature candy canes

Place popcorn in a large greased bowl or roasting pan; set aside. In a small bowl, combine the water, baking soda and vanilla; set aside. In a heavy saucepan, combine corn syrup and butter; heat over medium heat until butter is melted. Add sugar; cook and stir until sugar is dissolved and mixture comes to a boil. Cook and stir until a candy thermometer reaches 230° (thread stage), about 2 minutes.

Remove from the heat. Stir in vanilla mixture (mixture will foam) until blended. Immediately pour over popcorn, stirring to coat evenly. Cool for about 5 minutes, stirring several times. When cool enough to handle, firmly shape with buttered hands into 2-in. balls. Insert straight end of candy cane in the center of each ball. **Yield:** 2 dozen.

MACADAMIA FUDGE
Tina Jacobs, Wantage, New Jersey

There are few recipes I just have to pull out every holiday season, but this fudge is one. It couldn't be easier…or better!

1-1/2 teaspoons butter (no substitutes), softened
  3 cups (18 ounces) semisweet chocolate chips
  1 can (14 ounces) sweetened condensed milk
Pinch salt
  1 cup chopped macadamia nuts
1-1/2 teaspoons vanilla extract

Line an 8-in. square pan with foil and grease the foil with butter; set aside. In a heavy saucepan, combine the chocolate chips, milk and salt. Cook and stir over low heat until chips are melted. Remove from the heat; stir in nuts and vanilla. Pour into prepared pan. Chill for 2 hours or until firm. Using foil, lift fudge out of pan. Gently peel off foil; cut fudge into 1-in. squares. **Yield:** about 2 pounds.

SCRUMPTIOUS SWEETS. Savor and celebrate the season with treats that include Candy Cane Popcorn Balls, Walnut Caramel Treats and Sesame Toffee (p. 26, from top to bottom).

CHOCOLATE CHIP NOUGAT
Sandi Friest, Paynesville, Minnesota

This sweet, chewy nougat adds a pretty holiday blush to Yuletide gatherings. It takes a little extra effort to make, but candy this festive is worth it!

> 1 teaspoon plus 1/4 cup butter (no substitutes), softened, *divided*
> 3 cups sugar, *divided*
> 2/3 cup plus 1-1/4 cups light corn syrup, *divided*
> 2 tablespoons water
> 2 egg whites
> 2 cups chopped walnuts
> 2 teaspoons vanilla extract
> 1 cup miniature semisweet chocolate chips
> 2 to 3 drops red food coloring, optional

Line a 9-in. square pan with foil and grease the foil with 1 teaspoon butter; set aside. In a small heavy saucepan, combine 1 cup sugar, 2/3 cup corn syrup and water. Bring to a boil over medium heat, stirring constantly. Reduce heat to medium-low. Cook, without stirring, until a candy thermometer reads 238°.

Meanwhile, beat egg whites in a heat-proof mixing bowl until stiff peaks form. When the syrup reaches 238°, add it in a thin stream to egg whites, beating constantly at high speed until thick; cover and set aside.

In a large heavy saucepan, combine remaining sugar and corn syrup. Bring to a boil over medium heat, stirring constantly. Reduce heat to medium-low; cook, without stirring, until a candy thermometer reads 275° (soft-crack stage). Meanwhile, melt remaining butter. Pour hot syrup all at once into reserved egg white mixture; mix with a wooden spoon. Stir in the walnuts, melted butter and vanilla.

Pour half of the nougat mixture into prepared pan; press evenly. Sprinkle with chocolate chips. If desired, stir food coloring into remaining nougat mixture; turn into pan over chocolate chips. Press down evenly with buttered fingers. Let stand for several hours until set. Using foil, lift nougat out of pan. Discard foil; cut nougat into 1-in. squares. Wrap individually in waxed paper or foil; twist ends. **Yield:** 3 pounds.

CANDIED GRAPEFRUIT PEEL
Edna Everitt, Melbourne, Florida

My mother always made this fruity holiday sweet—and so do I. It takes time, but the house is filled with a "Christmasy" aroma while the grapefruit cools—and the candied sticks are simply delicious!

> 3 medium grapefruit
> 1 teaspoon salt
> 2 cups sugar, *divided*
> 1 cup water

With a sharp knife, score grapefruit peel into 8 to 10 wedge-shaped sections. Loosen peel with a tablespoon. With a small sharp knife, carefully remove white pith from peel. (Save fruit for another use.) In a large saucepan, combine peel and salt; cover with water. Bring to a boil. Reduce heat; simmer, uncovered, for 20 minutes. Drain. Repeat process twice (only covering with water and not adding more salt). Cool for 10 minutes. Cut peel into 1/4- to 1/2-in. strips; set aside.

In the same saucepan, combine 1-1/2 cups sugar and 1 cup water. Cook and stir until sugar is dissolved and mixture comes to a boil. Cook and stir for 2 minutes. Add grapefruit peel. Return to a boil. Reduce heat; simmer, uncovered, for 35-38 minutes or until syrup is almost absorbed and peel is transparent, stirring occasionally (watch carefully to prevent scorching).

Drain any remaining syrup. Cool peel in a single layer on a foil-lined baking sheet for at least 2-1/2 hours. Sprinkle with the remaining sugar if needed. **Yield:** about 1-1/2 cups.

ORANGE SPICED ALMONDS
Karen Paumen, Buffalo, Minnesota

After snacking on these tangy nuts at a local fair, I searched my cookbooks for a similar recipe. It took several trials, but now these sugar-and-spicy treats are a tradition!

> 2/3 cup sugar
> 3 teaspoons grated orange peel
> 1 teaspoon ground cinnamon
> 1/2 teaspoon ground allspice
> 1/2 teaspoon ground ginger
> 1 egg white
> 1 tablespoon orange juice
> 3 cups whole unblanched almonds

In a small bowl, combine the sugar, orange peel, cinnamon, allspice and ginger. In a small mixing bowl, beat egg white and orange juice. Add almonds; stir to coat. Sprinkle sugar mixture over almonds; mix well. Spread in a single layer on a baking sheet. Bake at 300° for 20 minutes. Remove to waxed paper to cool. **Yield:** about 3-1/2 cups.

NUTTY CHOCOLATE NUGGETS
Joann Wolfe, Toledo, Washington

My family can't get enough of these chewy, chocolaty drop cookies. They're so quick and easy to fix that I can whip up several batches even during the busy holiday season.

> 1/4 cup butter (no substitutes), softened
> 1/2 cup sugar
> 1 egg
> 1-1/2 teaspoons vanilla extract
> 1-1/2 squares (1-1/2 ounces) unsweetened chocolate, melted and cooled
> 1/2 cup all-purpose flour
> 1/4 teaspoon baking powder
> 1/2 teaspoon salt
> 2 cups chopped walnuts *or* pecans

In a mixing bowl, cream butter and sugar. Beat in egg and vanilla. Stir in chocolate. Combine the flour, baking powder and salt; gradually add to chocolate mixture. Stir in the nuts. Drop by rounded teaspoonfuls 2 in. apart onto ungreased baking sheets. Bake at 350° for 10-11 minutes or until edges are firm. Remove to wire racks to cool. **Yield:** about 3-1/2 dozen.

HONEY CREAM TAFFY
Iliene Taylor, Kearns, Utah

An old-fashioned favorite, this golden taffy gets my whole family pulling together in a special way! We wrap the melt-in-your-mouth confections in twists of waxed paper and give them out to our holiday visitors.

  1 tablespoon butter (no substitutes), softened
  1 cup whipping cream
  2 cups honey
  1 cup sugar

Grease a 15-in. x 10-in. x 1-in. baking pan with butter; place in the refrigerator. In a large deep heavy saucepan, combine cream and honey. Add sugar; cook over medium heat and stir with a wooden spoon until sugar is melted and mixture comes to a boil.

If sugar crystals are present, cover pan and boil for 1 minute. Uncover; cook, without stirring, until a candy thermometer reaches 290° (soft-crack stage). Remove from the heat and pour into prepared pan (do not scrape sides of saucepan). Cool for 5 minutes. Using a spoon, bring edges of honey mixture into center of pan. Cool 5-10 minutes longer or until cool enough to handle.

Using buttered hands, pull and stretch taffy until ridges form. (Taffy will lose its gloss and become light tan in color.) Pull into ropes about 1/2 in. thick. With a buttered kitchen scissors, cut into 1-in. pieces. Wrap individually in waxed paper. **Yield:** about 5 dozen.

CHERRY PEANUT BUTTER BALLS
Leora Muellerleile, Turtle Lake, Wisconsin

Years ago, I saved this festive recipe and made it only at Christmastime. But my grandkids loved the sweet combination of peanut butter, chocolate and cherries so much that now I mix up a batch anytime they ask or visit!

1/2 cup butter (no substitutes), softened
  1 cup peanut butter*
  1 teaspoon vanilla extract
  2 cups confectioners' sugar
  24 to 26 maraschino cherries
Additional confectioners' sugar
  2 cups (12 ounce) semisweet chocolate chips
1/4 cup shortening

In a small mixing bowl, cream the butter, peanut butter and vanilla; mix well. Gradually beat in confectioners' sugar. Cover and refrigerate for at least 1 hour.

Pat cherries dry with paper towel. Dust hands with additional confectioners' sugar.

Wrap each cherry with a rounded tablespoonful of peanut butter mixture; shape into a ball. (Peanut butter mixture may need to be refrigerated occasionally while rolling cherries.) Cover and refrigerate for at least 1 hour.

In a microwave or heavy saucepan, melt chocolate chips and shortening; stir until smooth.

Dip the peanut butter balls in chocolate; place on waxed paper. Refrigerate for at least 1 hour or until set. **Yield:** about 2 dozen.

*Editor's Note: Reduced-fat or generic brands of peanut butter are not recommended for this recipe.

CHOCOLATE ZEBRA CLUSTERS
Paige Scott, Murfreesboro, Tennessee

Just one bite and chocolate lovers will melt over these yummy clusters filled with salted nuts, rice cereal and marshmallows! And they're so pretty, no one can believe how easy they are.

  2 cups (12 ounces) semisweet chocolate chips
  12 ounces white candy coating, *divided*
1-1/4 cups salted peanuts
1-1/4 cups crisp rice cereal
2-1/4 cups miniature marshmallows
  1 teaspoon shortening

Line two baking sheets with waxed paper; set aside. In a large microwave-safe bowl, melt chips and 7 ounces white candy coating at 70% power; stir until smooth. Stir in peanuts and cereal. Cool slightly; fold in marshmallows. Drop by rounded tablespoonfuls onto prepared baking sheets.

In another microwave-safe bowl, melt shortening and remaining candy coating; stir until smooth. Transfer to a pastry or plastic bag; cut a small hole in the corner of bag. Drizzle over clusters. Refrigerate for 5 minutes or until set. Store in an airtight container. **Yield:** 2-1/2 dozen.

CHOCOLATE ALMOND BARS
Jackie Hannahs, Fountain, Wisconsin

Loaded with almond flavor, these chewy bars are one of my husband's favorite sweet treats.

1-1/2 cups all-purpose flour
  2/3 cup sugar
  3/4 cup cold butter *or* margarine
  1 can (14 ounces) sweetened condensed milk
1-1/2 cups semisweet chocolate chips, *divided*
  1 egg, beaten
  2 cups chopped almonds, toasted
  1/4 teaspoon almond extract
  1 teaspoon shortening

In a bowl, combine the flour and sugar; cut in butter until crumbly. Press into a greased 13-in. x 9-in. x 2-in. baking pan. Bake at 350° for 18-20 minutes or until lightly browned. Cool on a wire rack.

In a saucepan, combine the milk and 1 cup chocolate chips. Cook and stir over low heat until chips are melted. Remove from the heat; cool slightly. Stir in egg, almonds and extract. Spread over crust. Bake at 350° for 20-25 minutes or until a toothpick inserted near the center comes out clean. Cool on a wire rack. In a microwave, melt shortening and remaining chips; drizzle over top. Cut into bars. **Yield:** 4 dozen.

Editor's Note: We recommend that you test your candy thermometer before each use by bringing water to a boil; the thermometer should read 212°. Adjust your recipe temperature up or down based on your own test.

Appetizers

Make your Yuletide gathering merry and bright with this showstopping spread of fun finger foods, hearty party snacks and tempting taste-teasers.

SWEET 'N' SOUR SAUSAGE
Mary Poninski, Whittington, Illinois
(Pictured on page 30)

A sweet sauce and merry Christmas colors make this fruit-and-sausage combo a trusted holiday crowd-pleaser. Hearty enough to serve for brunch, it always disappears in a twinkling!

2 cans (8 ounces *each*) pineapple chunks
2 tablespoons cornstarch
1/2 teaspoon salt
1/2 cup maple syrup
1/3 cup water
1/3 cup cider vinegar
1 large green pepper, cut into 1-inch pieces
2 packages (8 ounces *each*) brown-and-serve sausage links
1/2 cup red maraschino cherries, halved

Drain the pineapple, reserving juice. Set the pineapple and juice aside. In a large saucepan, combine the cornstarch, salt, maple syrup, water, vinegar and reserved pineapple juice until smooth. Bring to a boil; cook and stir for 2 minutes or until thickened. Add the green pepper; cook 2 minutes longer.

Meanwhile, in a skillet, brown sausage; drain. Cut each link into thirds. Add the sausage, cherries and reserved pineapple to saucepan; heat through. **Yield:** 4-6 servings.

CHRISTMAS CHEESE BALLS
Margie Cadwell, Eastman, Georgia
(Pictured on page 30)

Christmas at our house just wouldn't be complete without these rich cheese balls. Friends and family ask for them every year—and I can make three gifts from just one recipe.

4 packages (8 ounces *each*) cream cheese, softened
4 cups (1 pound) shredded cheddar cheese
1 cup chopped pecans
1/4 cup evaporated milk
1 can (2-1/4 ounces) chopped ripe olives, drained
2 garlic cloves, minced
1/2 teaspoon salt
Minced fresh parsley, chopped pecans and paprika
Assorted crackers

In a small mixing bowl, beat the cream cheese and cheddar cheese. Stir in the pecans, milk, olives, garlic and salt. Divide into thirds; roll each into a ball. Roll one ball in parsley and one in nuts. Sprinkle one with paprika. Cover and refrigerate. Remove from the refrigerator 15 minutes before serving. Serve with crackers. **Yield:** 3 cheese balls.

AWESOME APPETIZERS. Any hungry holiday crowd would enjoy this array of Sweet 'n' Sour Sausage, Christmas Cheese Balls and a Snow Pea Holiday Wreath (p. 30, clockwise from upper left).

SNOW PEA HOLIDAY WREATH
Carol Schneck, Stockton, California
(Pictured on page 30)

Santa himself might stop to sample this pretty-as-a-picture finger food! Crunchy green pea pods and juicy red tomatoes add a naturally fresh, festive holiday note to my buffet table.

1 package (3 ounces) cream cheese, softened
1/4 teaspoon garlic powder
1/4 teaspoon seasoned salt
1/2 pound fresh snow peas, strings removed
2 cups grape or cherry tomatoes

In a small mixing bowl, combine the cream cheese, garlic powder and seasoned salt. Place mixture in a pastry bag or heavy-duty plastic bag with a small star tip. Pipe about 1/4 teaspoon of mixture onto the wide end of each pea pod. Arrange pods on a serving platter with cheese mixture toward the outside of the platter; fill center with tomatoes. **Yield:** 20 servings.

SAUERKRAUT MEATBALLS
Christine Batts, Murray, Kentucky

This zesty recipe is a great way to pep up a party! The hot pork sausage and sauerkraut make terrific-tasting meatballs, and the mustard dipping sauce is a nice complement.

1/2 pound bulk hot pork sausage
1/4 cup finely chopped onion
1 can (14 ounces) sauerkraut, rinsed, drained and finely chopped
2 tablespoons plus 3/4 cup dry bread crumbs, *divided*
1 package (3 ounces) cream cheese, softened
2 tablespoons minced fresh parsley
1/2 teaspoon ground mustard
1/4 teaspoon garlic salt
1/8 teaspoon pepper
1/4 cup all-purpose flour
2 eggs
1/4 cup milk
Oil for deep-fat frying
1/2 cup mayonnaise
2 tablespoons spicy brown mustard

In a skillet, cook sausage and onion over medium heat until meat is no longer pink and onion is tender; drain. Stir in sauerkraut and 2 tablespoons bread crumbs; set aside. In a small mixing bowl, combine the cream cheese, parsley, mustard, garlic salt and pepper; stir into sauerkraut mixture. Cover and refrigerate for at least 1 hour or overnight.

Shape into 3/4-in. balls; roll in flour. In a small bowl, beat eggs and milk. Dip meatballs into egg mixture, then roll in remaining bread crumbs. In an electric skillet, heat 2 in. of oil to 375°. Fry meatballs until golden brown; drain. Combine mayonnaise and mustard; serve with meatballs. Refrigerate leftovers. **Yield:** about 2 dozen.

APPETIZER CRAB PIZZA
Heidi Ralston, Tionesta, Pennsylvania

Guests will know you fussed when they bite into a wedge of this rich, golden pizza with a made-from-scratch crust. Cream cheese, crabmeat and herbs make up the yummy topping.

>　3 to 3-1/2 cups all-purpose flour
>　1 package (1/4 ounce) active dry yeast
>　1 teaspoon sugar
> 1/2 teaspoon salt
>　1 cup water
>　2 tablespoons olive *or* vegetable oil
> TOPPINGS:
>　2 packages (8 ounces *each*) cream cheese, softened
>　2 cans (6 ounces *each*) crabmeat, drained, flaked and cartilage removed *or* 2 cups chopped imitation crabmeat
> 1/4 cup milk
>　1 cup (4 ounces) crumbled feta cheese
>　1 teaspoon dried basil
>　1 teaspoon dried oregano
> 1/2 teaspoon garlic powder
>　1 cup (4 ounces) shredded Swiss cheese, *divided*

In a large mixing bowl, combine 1-1/2 cups flour, yeast, sugar and salt. In a saucepan, heat water and oil to 120°-130°. Add to dry ingredients; beat on medium speed for 3 minutes. Stir in enough remaining flour to form a soft dough. Turn onto a floured surface; knead until smooth and elastic, about 8 minutes. Place in a greased bowl, turning once to grease top. Cover and let rise in a warm place until doubled, about 1 hour.

Punch dough down; divide in half. On a floured surface, roll each piece into a 13-in. circle; transfer to two 12-in. pizza pans. Build up edge slightly. Prick dough thoroughly with a fork. Bake crusts at 450° for 10-12 minutes or until lightly browned. Combine the cream cheese, crab, milk, feta cheese, basil, oregano and garlic powder; spread half of the mixture over each crust. Sprinkle each with 1/2 cup Swiss cheese. Bake 10-12 minutes longer or until crust is golden and cheese is melted. Cut into wedges. **Yield:** 2 pizzas (8-10 servings each).

SNOW PUNCH
Eloise Neeley, Norton, Ohio

As pretty as a fresh snowdrift, this frothy, fruity punch has been a Christmas tradition in our family for years—but it's a light and refreshing thirst-quencher in any season.

>　1 cup lemon juice
>　5 medium ripe bananas
>　1 cup sugar
>　2 cups half-and-half cream
>　1 liter lemon-lime soda, chilled
>　1 pint lemon *or* pineapple sherbet
> 1/4 cup flaked coconut, optional

In a blender or food processor, cover and process the lemon juice, bananas and sugar. Add cream; blend until smooth. Cover and refrigerate. Just before serving, pour banana mixture into a punch bowl. Stir in soda. Top with lemon sherbet and coconut if desired. **Yield:** 2-1/2 quarts.

CREAMY HERB SLICES
Kelly Schulz, Oak Forest, Illinois

These dressed-up slices of French bread go well with soup or salad...or can be served as an appetizer. I have to move fast after putting them out—or there are none left for me!

>　1 package (8 ounces) cream cheese, softened
>　1 tablespoon minced fresh parsley
>　1 tablespoon minced chives
>　2 teaspoons chopped green onion
>　2 garlic cloves, minced
>　1 teaspoon dill weed
> 1/2 teaspoon pepper
>　1 loaf (1/2 pound) French bread

In a small bowl, combine the first seven ingredients. Cut bread into 1/2-in. slices; spread each slice with 1 tablespoon cream cheese mixture. Place on ungreased baking sheets. Bake at 400° for 7 minutes or broil for 2 minutes or until golden brown. **Yield:** about 22 appetizers.

PARTY BARBECUED FRANKS
Dorothy Anderson, Ottawa, Kansas

These peachy little franks disappear quickly whenever I serve them. The sweet and tangy sauce appeals to all ages.

>　2 teaspoons cornstarch
>　2 tablespoons cold water
>　1 jar (18 ounces) peach preserves
>　1 cup barbecue sauce
>　2 packages (1 pound *each*) miniature hot dogs *or* smoked sausage

In a large saucepan, combine the cornstarch and water until smooth. Stir in the preserves and barbecue sauce. Bring to a boil; cook and stir for 2 minutes or until thickened. Stir in hot dogs until coated. Cover and cook for 5 minutes or until heated through. **Yield:** 20 servings.

CRAB-STUFFED DEVILED EGGS
Inez Orsburn, De Motte, Indiana

For a little something special, I like to include this appealing appetizer in holiday buffets. Guests really go for the creamy crab filling with almonds and celery that add a fun crunch.

> 12 hard-cooked eggs
>　1 can (6 ounces) crabmeat, drained, flaked and cartilage removed *or* 1 cup finely chopped imitation crabmeat
> 2/3 cup mayonnaise
> 1/2 cup finely chopped celery
> 1/2 cup chopped slivered almonds
>　2 tablespoons finely chopped green pepper
> 1/2 teaspoon salt

Slice eggs in half lengthwise. Remove yolks and set whites aside. In a bowl, mash yolks. Stir in the crab, mayonnaise, celery, almonds, green pepper and salt. Stuff or pipe into egg whites. Refrigerate until ready to serve. **Yield:** 2 dozen.

TASTY TORTILLA ROLL-UPS
J. O'Neall, Westminster, Colorado

Celebrate the season in Southwest style with these tasty pin-wheel roll-ups. They're simple to make, easy for guests to handle and look so colorful on a serving tray or buffet table.

>   2 packages (one 8 ounces, one 3 ounces) cream
>   cheese, softened
>   1/4 cup minced green onions
>   3 tablespoons chopped green chilies *or* jalapeno
>   peppers
>   3 tablespoons chopped ripe olives
>   3 tablespoons diced pimientos, drained
>   3 tablespoons finely chopped pecans *or* walnuts
>   1/8 teaspoon garlic powder
>   5 flour tortillas (8 inches)

In a small mixing bowl, beat cream cheese. Stir in green onions, green chilies, olives, pimientos, pecans and garlic powder. Spread over tortillas. Roll up tightly. Wrap in plastic wrap. Refrigerate for at least 2 hours. Cut into 1/2-in. pieces. **Yield:** 2-1/2 dozen.

   Editor's Note: When cutting or seeding hot peppers, use rubber or plastic gloves to protect your hands. Avoid touching your face.

CHEESY PARTY PUFFS
JoAnn Rohde, Vestal, New York

The first time I made these puffs for friends, all eight couples asked for the recipe! They're so tasty and quick to make in this busy season—and everyone loves them.

>   1 tube (7-1/2 ounces) refrigerated buttermilk
>   biscuits
>   5 pieces (5 ounces) string cheese, cut into fourths
>   3 to 4 tablespoons prepared Italian salad dressing
>   1/4 cup grated Parmesan cheese
>   Pizza sauce *or* ranch salad dressing, optional

Cut each biscuit in half; flatten each piece into a 2-1/2-in. circle. Place a piece of cheese in the center of each. Bring dough around cheese; pinch edges to seal. Roll in salad dressing. Dip the top of each ball in Parmesan cheese; place seam side down on a greased baking sheet. Bake at 375° for 8-10 minutes or until golden brown. Serve with pizza sauce or ranch dressing if desired. **Yield:** 5 servings.

TANGY PORK MEATBALLS
Katie Koziolek, Hartland, Minnesota

Yuletide buffet "grazers" stampede for these meatballs! The mouth-watering morsels go so fast, I often make several batches at once. Barbecue sauce adds a nice bite to the mildly seasoned ground pork.

>   2 eggs, beaten
>   2/3 cup dried bread crumbs
>   2 tablespoons dried minced onion
>   2 teaspoons seasoned salt
>   2 pounds ground pork

SAUCE:
>   1-1/2 cups ketchup
>   1 can (8 ounces) tomato sauce
>   3 tablespoons Worcestershire sauce
>   2 to 3 tablespoons cider vinegar
>   2 teaspoons liquid smoke, optional

In a bowl, combine the eggs, bread crumbs, onion and salt. Crumble pork over mixture and mix well. Shape into 3/4-in. balls; place on a greased 15-in. x 10-in. x 1-in. baking pan. Bake at 400° for 15 minutes or until the meat is no longer pink.

   Meanwhile in a large saucepan, combine sauce ingredients. Simmer, uncovered, for 10 minutes, stirring occasionally. Add meatballs. Serve in a slow cooker or chafing dish. **Yield:** about 1-1/2 dozen.

SIX-LAYER DIP
Etta Gillespie, San Angelo, Texas
(Pictured below)

Tortilla chips make great scoopers for this dip, which is a family favorite after we open Christmas gifts. Sometimes I serve it in a glass bowl—just to show off the pretty layers.

>   2 medium ripe avocados, peeled and sliced
>   2 tablespoons lemon juice
>   1/2 teaspoon garlic salt
>   1/8 teaspoon hot pepper sauce
>   1 cup (8 ounces) sour cream
>   1 can (2-1/4 ounces) chopped ripe olives, drained
>   1 jar (16 ounces) thick and chunky salsa, drained
>   2 medium tomatoes, seeded and chopped
>   1 cup (4 ounces) shredded cheddar cheese
>   Tortilla chips

In a bowl, combine the avocados, lemon juice, garlic salt and hot pepper sauce; mash well. Spoon into a deep-dish 10-in. pie plate or serving bowl. Layer with sour cream, olives, salsa, tomatoes and cheese. Cover and refrigerate for at least 1 hour. Serve with chips. **Yield:** 20 servings.

Christmas Dinner

DELECTABLE DINING. This holiday feast includes (clockwise fom top left): Stuffed Bone-In Ham (p. 36), Chocolate Peanut Butter Cheesecake (p. 37), Orange-Cranberry Tossed Salad (p. 36), Glazed Whole Beets (p. 36) and Corn Spoon Bread (p. 36).

There's no place like home for the holidays. These festive recipes will help you celebrate with family and friends who gather near to share the spirit of this joyous season!

STUFFED BONE-IN HAM
Rebecca Watts, Laneville, Texas
(Pictured on page 34)

Scored with a simple but delicious stuffing, this glazed ham makes such an elegant statement when you set it on your holiday table! It's become a Yuletide tradition at our house.

   1 medium onion, finely chopped
1/2 cup finely chopped celery
   2 tablespoons minced fresh parsley
1/2 cup butter *or* margarine
1/4 cup egg substitute
3/4 cup milk
   1 teaspoon rubbed sage
1/2 teaspoon dried thyme
1/4 teaspoon salt
   6 cups soft bread cubes (1/4-inch cubes)
   1 shank half bone-in fully cooked ham
     (about 12 pounds)
GLAZE:
1/2 cup packed brown sugar
1/4 cup orange juice
1/4 cup dark corn syrup

In a large skillet, saute the onion, celery and parsley in butter until vegetables are tender. In a bowl, combine the egg substitute, milk, sage, thyme and salt. Add bread cubes and vegetable mixture; toss to combine.

From the cut end of the ham, cut five parallel wedges, about 1-1/2 in. apart, 1/2 in. wide and 1-1/2 in. deep. Repeat in the opposite direction, making diamond shapes. Spoon stuffing into slits. Place ham on a rack in a shallow roasting pan. Cover loosely with a foil tent. Bake at 325° for 2-1/4 hours.

In a saucepan, combine the glaze ingredients. Cook and stir over medium heat until sugar is dissolved. Remove foil from ham; drizzle glaze over top. Bake 30-45 minutes longer or until a meat thermometer reads 140°. Let stand for 10 minutes before slicing. **Yield:** 15-18 servings.

ORANGE-CRANBERRY TOSSED SALAD
Bernice Weir, Hot Springs Village, Arkansas
(Pictured on page 35)

Candied cranberries and mandarin oranges sparkle like jewels in this merry Christmas salad my family's enjoyed for years.

   2 cups fresh *or* frozen cranberries, thawed
   1 cup sugar
   3 tablespoons orange juice
   2 tablespoons cider vinegar
   2 tablespoons honey
   1 teaspoon poppy seeds
   1 teaspoon ground mustard
Dash salt and pepper
3/4 cup vegetable oil
   2 heads Boston *or* Bibb lettuce, torn
   1 can (11 ounces) mandarin oranges, drained

For candied cranberries, place cranberries in a baking pan; sprinkle with sugar. Cover tightly with foil and bake at 350° for 30 minutes, stirring every 15 minutes. Place in a single layer on greased aluminum foil; cool for at least 30 minutes.

For salad dressing, combine the orange juice, vinegar, honey, poppy seeds, mustard, salt and pepper in a small bowl. Slowly whisk in oil. Just before serving, toss lettuce, oranges and dressing in a large bowl. Sprinkle with candied cranberries. **Yield:** 12 servings.

GLAZED WHOLE BEETS
Sylvia Lepczyk, Pittsburgh, Pennsylvania
(Pictured on page 34)

This recipe came from my mother and was always a favorite holiday side dish when I was growing up. The glaze is such a wonderfully quick and easy way to dress up canned beets.

   3 cans (15 ounces *each*) whole beets
   5 teaspoons sugar
   1 tablespoon all-purpose flour
1/4 teaspoon salt
   1 tablespoon cider vinegar

Drain beets, reserving 2/3 cup juice. In a large skillet, combine the sugar, flour and salt. Stir in vinegar and reserved beet juice until smooth. Bring to a boil; cook and stir for 2 minutes or until thickened. Add beets; reduce heat. Cook, uncovered, for 4-5 minutes or until heated through. **Yield:** 6 servings.

CORN SPOON BREAD
Ruth Campbell, Staunton, Virginia
(Pictured on page 34)

Here's a comforting side dish that has saved quite a few ordinary meals at our house. To spice it up a bit for Christmas, I stir in a can of holly-green chopped chilies. It's as good for breakfast as it is at lunch or dinner.

   3 eggs, *separated*
1-1/2 cups milk
3/4 cup cornmeal
3/4 teaspoon salt
   1 can (14-3/4 ounces) cream-style corn
   2 tablespoons butter *or* margarine, softened
3/4 teaspoon baking powder

In a mixing bowl, beat egg whites until stiff peaks form; set aside. In another bowl, beat egg yolks; set aside. In a saucepan, bring milk to a boil. Add cornmeal and salt. Reduce heat; cook and stir for 1 minute or until thickened. Remove from the heat. Stir in the corn, butter and baking powder. Stir in egg yolks. Fold in egg whites.

Transfer to a greased 11-in. x 7-in. x 2-in. baking dish. Bake, uncovered, at 350° for 30-35 minutes or just until set. Serve immediately with a spoon. **Yield:** 6-8 servings.

CHOCOLATE PEANUT BUTTER CHEESECAKE

Mrs. H.L. Sosnowski, Grand Island, New York
(Pictured on page 35)

Family and friends always "ooh" and "aah" when I bring out this tempting cheesecake after holiday dinners! Filled with peanut butter and cream cheese and drizzled with chocolate in a fudge crust, it's a showstopper.

BROWNIE CRUST:
1/4 cup butter (no substitutes)
3 squares (1 ounce *each*) unsweetened chocolate
1 cup packed brown sugar
2 eggs
1-1/2 teaspoons vanilla extract
2/3 cup all-purpose flour
1/8 teaspoon baking powder
1 square (1 ounce) semisweet chocolate, chopped
FILLING:
1 jar (12 ounces) creamy peanut butter
2 packages (one 8 ounces, one 3 ounces) cream cheese, softened
1 cup packed brown sugar
3 eggs
1/2 cup sour cream
TOPPING:
3/4 cup sour cream
2 teaspoons sugar
Melted semisweet chocolate, optional

In a microwave, melt butter and unsweetened chocolate; set aside. In a mixing bowl, beat brown sugar and eggs until light and fluffy, about 4 minutes. Add chocolate mixture and vanilla; mix well. Combine flour and baking powder; add to batter. Stir in chopped chocolate. Spread 1 cup into a greased 9-in. springform pan. Cover and refrigerate remaining batter. Place pan on a baking sheet. Bake at 350° for 17-19 minutes or until a toothpick inserted near the center comes out clean. Cool on a wire rack for 5 minutes; place in freezer for 15 minutes.

For filling, in a mixing bowl, beat peanut butter, cream cheese and brown sugar until smooth. Add eggs and sour cream; beat on low speed just until combined. Spread remaining brownie batter about 1-1/2 in. high around sides of pan, sealing to baked crust. Pour filling into center. Bake at 350° for 45 minutes or until center is almost set.

For topping, combine sour cream and sugar; spread over filling to within 3/4 in. of edges. Return cheesecake to the oven; turn oven off and let stand for 5 minutes. Cool on a wire rack for 10 minutes. Carefully run a knife around pan to loosen; cool 1 hour longer. Chill overnight. Remove sides of pan. Drizzle top with melted chocolate. Refrigerate leftovers. **Yield:** 12 servings.

NEAPOLITAN POTATOES

Kristi Beneschan, Lincoln, Nebraska

One taste of these yummy potatoes and I pestered my friend for months to give me the recipe! The tantalizing blend of flavors complements any festive entree.

1/2 cup grated Parmesan cheese
3 garlic cloves, minced

1/2 cup minced fresh basil
1/4 cup minced fresh parsley
2 teaspoons minced fresh oregano
1-1/2 teaspoons salt
1 teaspoon pepper
7 tablespoons olive *or* vegetable oil, *divided*
6 cups thinly sliced red potatoes (about 2 pounds)
1 can (14-1/2 ounces) diced tomatoes, drained

In a bowl, combine the first seven ingredients; set aside. Grease a shallow 2-1/2-qt. baking dish with 1 tablespoon oil. Place a third of the potatoes and tomatoes in dish. Drizzle with 2 tablespoons oil; sprinkle with a third of the cheese mixture. Repeat layers twice. Cover and bake at 350° for 55-65 minutes or until the potatoes are tender. **Yield:** 6-8 servings.

WHITE CHOCOLATE BREAD PUDDING

Wendy Sleicher, Quakertown, Pennsylvania

This delectable dessert features vanilla chips, apples and a sweet caramel sauce. It's a favorite with our boys.

2 cups milk
2 cups whipping cream
1 cup sugar
1 cup vanilla *or* white chips
8 eggs
1 tablespoon vanilla extract
1 loaf (1 pound) egg bread, crust removed, cut into 1-inch cubes
2 medium tart apples, peeled and chopped
CARAMEL SAUCE:
1-1/4 cups sugar
1/2 cup water
1/4 cup light corn syrup
1 tablespoon lemon juice
1-1/4 cups whipping cream
1 cup chopped pecans, toasted
2 teaspoons vanilla extract

In a saucepan, combine the milk, cream and sugar. Cook over medium heat until mixture comes to a boil. Remove from the heat; stir in chips until melted. In a bowl, whisk eggs and vanilla. Gradually whisk in cream mixture. Add bread. Let stand for 15 minutes, stirring occasionally.

Stir in apples. Pour into a greased 13-in. x 9-in. x 2-in. baking dish. Cover and bake at 350° for 45 minutes. Uncover; bake 30 minutes longer or until a knife inserted near the center comes out clean.

Meanwhile, for sauce, combine the sugar, water, corn syrup and lemon juice in a large saucepan. Cook and stir over medium heat until sugar is dissolved. Bring to a boil over medium-high heat; boil, without stirring, until a candy thermometer reads 295° and mixture turns deep amber.

Remove from the heat; stir in cream. Cook and stir over low heat until mixture is smooth. Bring to a boil over medium heat; cook and stir for 4 minutes. Stir in nuts and vanilla. Stir before serving. Serve warm over warm bread pudding. **Yield:** 12-15 servings.

Editor's Note: We recommend that you test your candy thermometer before each use by bringing water to a boil; the thermometer should read 212°. Adjust your recipe temperature up or down based on your test.

SWEDISH MEATBALLS
Ruth Andrewson, Leavenworth, Washington

I can still remember Mother making this delicious recipe in an old iron skillet on her wood-burning stove years ago. It's such wonderful family fare, we still enjoy warming up with it on cold winter nights!

1 egg
1/2 cup milk
3/4 cup dry bread crumbs
3/4 cup finely chopped onion
1 teaspoon Worcestershire sauce
1 teaspoon salt
1/2 to 3/4 teaspoon ground allspice
1/4 teaspoon pepper
1-1/2 pounds ground beef
3/4 pound ground pork
1 tablespoon vegetable oil
1 can (10-3/4 ounces) condensed cream of mushroom soup, undiluted
1/2 cup water
Hot cooked noodles

In a bowl, combine the first eight ingredients. Crumble meat over mixture; mix well. Shape into 1-1/2-in. balls. In a large skillet, brown meatballs in oil in small batches over medium heat; drain.

Place meatballs in a greased 2-qt. baking dish. Combine the soup and water; pour over the meatballs. Bake, uncovered, at 350° for about 40-45 minutes or until the meat is no longer pink. Serve over egg noodles. **Yield:** 10 servings.

SWEET POTATO APPLE DRESSING
Gail Prather, Bethel, Minnesota

This dressing is simply the greatest. It's easy to make, creates a heavenly aroma when baking and combines two traditional favorites—sweet potatoes and dressing—into one special dish. Folks always give it rave reviews.

1-1/2 cups chopped green onions
2 celery ribs, chopped
1/2 cup butter *or* margarine
3 cups diced cooked sweet potatoes
3 medium tart apples, peeled and diced
4 cups soft bread cubes
1/2 cup chopped walnuts
3 eggs, lightly beaten
1/4 cup minced fresh parsley
2 teaspoons dried thyme
1 teaspoon rubbed sage
1/2 teaspoon salt
1/2 teaspoon pepper
1/4 teaspoon ground nutmeg

In a skillet, saute onions and celery in butter until tender. Transfer to a large bowl; add the sweet potatoes, apples, bread cubes and walnuts. Add eggs; toss to coat. Stir in the remaining ingredients. Spoon into a greased 2-1/2-qt. baking dish. Cover and bake at 350° for 40 minutes. Uncover; bake 10 minutes longer or until lightly browned. **Yield:** 10-12 servings.

SWISS BEAN CASSEROLE
Eleanor McCutcheon, Monticello, Florida

This delicious creamy and cheesy side dish is too rich to serve often, so I save it for Christmas—as a kind of reward for good behavior all year long!

2 tablespoons chopped onion
1/3 cup butter *or* margarine
1/3 cup all-purpose flour
1 teaspoon salt
1/2 teaspoon white pepper
1/2 teaspoon ground mustard
2 cups milk
1-1/2 cups (6 ounces) shredded Swiss cheese
1 package (16 ounces) frozen French-style green beans, thawed and drained
1/4 cup slivered almonds, toasted

In a large saucepan, saute onion in butter until tender. Stir in the flour, salt, pepper and mustard until blended. Gradually add milk. Bring to a boil; cook and stir for 2 minutes or until thickened and bubbly. Reduce heat to low; stir in cheese just until melted.

Stir in beans until coated. Transfer to a greased 2-qt. baking dish. Sprinkle with almonds. Bake, uncovered, at 350° for 25-30 minutes or until bubbly. **Yield:** 6-8 servings.

FESTIVE PEA SALAD
J. O'Neall, Westminster, Colorado

Colorful and dressed up enough for Christmas, here's an easy-to-make salad that is wonderful all year-round. The green peas and red onion make it especially festive looking.

1 package (16 ounces) frozen petite peas, thawed
1-1/2 cups fresh snow peas, trimmed and halved
1 cup halved thinly sliced red onion
1 jar (2 ounces) diced pimientos, drained
1/3 cup mayonnaise
1/3 cup sour cream
1 teaspoon minced fresh mint
1/4 teaspoon salt
1/8 teaspoon white pepper
Dash to 1/8 teaspoon ground nutmeg
5 bacon strips, cooked and crumbled

In a large bowl, combine the peas, onion and pimientos. In a small bowl, combine the mayonnaise, sour cream, mint, salt, pepper and nutmeg. Pour over pea mixture; toss to coat. Cover and refrigerate for at least 1 hour. Just before serving, stir in the bacon. **Yield:** 8-10 servings.

● Lighting and music can wrap up any holiday gathering in a festive and relaxing atmosphere. Try groupings of bright votive candles or different-sized pillars on a mirrored surface to show off your spread (and your guests) in the best light. For music, what could be nicer than the sounds of the season? Mix instrumental with vocal carols.

SHRIMP IN CREAM SAUCE
Jane Birch, Edison, New Jersey
(Pictured at right)

Looking for an extra-special Christmas Eve entree to delight your busy crowd? My family always manages to make time for this rich shrimp dish. We enjoy it over golden egg noodles.

2 tablespoons butter *or* margarine, melted
1/3 cup all-purpose flour
1-1/2 cups chicken broth
4 garlic cloves, minced
1 cup whipping cream
1/2 cup minced fresh parsley
2 teaspoons paprika
Salt and pepper to taste
2 pounds large uncooked shrimp, peeled and deveined
Hot cooked noodles *or* rice

In a saucepan, melt butter; stir in flour until smooth. Gradually add broth and garlic. Bring to a boil; cook and stir for 2 minutes or until thickened. Remove from the heat. Stir in the cream, parsley, paprika, salt and pepper.

Cut shrimp lengthwise but not all the way through; spread to butterfly. Place cut side down in a greased 13-in. x 9-in. x 2-in. baking dish. Pour cream sauce over shrimp. Bake, uncovered, at 400° for 15-18 minutes or until shrimp turn pink. Serve over noodles or rice. **Yield: 8 servings.**

CURRIED SQUASH SOUP
Evelyn Southwell, Etters, Pennsylvania

Cayenne pepper gives a little kick to bowls of this pretty golden soup, a first course that everyone seems to love. It can be made several days ahead to fit a busy schedule, then heated up whenever needed.

1 butternut squash (about 1-3/4 pounds)
1 large onion, chopped
2 garlic cloves, minced
2 tablespoons vegetable oil
1 tablespoon all-purpose flour
1 teaspoon salt
1 teaspoon curry powder
1/8 teaspoon cayenne pepper
5 cups chicken broth
1 bay leaf
CILANTRO CREAM TOPPING:
1/2 cup sour cream
1/4 cup whipping cream
1/4 cup minced fresh cilantro *or* parsley

Cut squash in half lengthwise; discard seeds. Place squash cut side down in a greased or foil-lined baking pan. Bake, uncovered, at 400° for 40-50 minutes or until tender. When cool enough to handle, scoop out pulp; set aside.

In a large saucepan, saute onion and garlic in oil until tender. Add the flour, salt, curry powder and cayenne until blended. Stir in broth. Add bay leaf. Bring to a boil; cook and stir for 2 minutes or until thickened. Reduce heat; simmer, uncovered, for 20 minutes. Discard bay leaf. Cool to room temperature.

In a blender or food processor, place half of the broth mixture and squash; cover and process until smooth. Repeat with remaining broth mixture and squash. Return to the saucepan; heat through. Combine the topping ingredients; place a dollop on each serving. **Yield: 6 servings.**

APRICOT-GLAZED PORK LOIN ROAST
Ramona Stude, Mineral Point, Wisconsin

A nice alternative for a special dinner during the Yuletide season or any other time of year, this pork roast gets its fruity flavor and lovely golden color from apricots. I serve it often to guests.

1 bone-in pork loin roast (4 to 5 pounds)
1/2 teaspoon salt
1/2 teaspoon pepper
2/3 cup packed brown sugar
2 tablespoons cornstarch
1-1/4 teaspoons ground mustard
2 cups apricot nectar
4 teaspoons cider vinegar

Sprinkle roast with salt and pepper. Place on a rack in a shallow roasting pan. Bake, uncovered, at 350° for 1-1/2 hours. In a saucepan, combine the brown sugar, cornstarch and mustard. Stir in apricot nectar and vinegar until smooth. Bring to a boil over medium heat; cook and stir for 2 minutes or until thickened.

Spoon 1/2 cup glaze over roast. Bake 20 minutes longer or until a meat thermometer reads 160°. Let stand for 10-15 minutes before slicing. Serve with remaining glaze. **Yield: 8 servings.**

Captivating Cookies

Make the season special for friends and family with this mouth-watering selection of homemade Christmas cookies, old-fashioned bars and other merry morsels!

FENNEL TEA COOKIES
Susan Beck, Napa, California
(Pictured on page 40)

These tender buttery tea cookies have a lovely fennel flavor and add a touch of elegance to any holiday cookie tray. Rolled in confectioners' sugar, they look like snowballs!

      1 tablespoon fennel seed, crushed
      2 tablespoons boiling water
  3/4 cup butter (no substitutes), softened
  2/3 cup packed brown sugar
      1 egg
      2 cups all-purpose flour
  1/2 teaspoon baking soda
Confectioners' sugar

In a small bowl, soak fennel seed in boiling water; set aside. In a mixing bowl, cream butter and brown sugar. Beat in egg. Drain fennel seed. Combine the flour, baking soda and fennel seed; gradually add to creamed mixture. Roll into 1-in. balls; place 2 in. apart on ungreased baking sheets. Bake at 350° for 10-12 minutes or until lightly browned. Roll warm cookies in confectioners' sugar. Cool on wire racks. **Yield:** 3 dozen.

PEANUT BUTTER CUTOUT COOKIES
Cindi Bauer, Marshfield, Wisconsin
(Pictured on page 40)

Here's a nice change of pace from the more traditional sugar cutouts. And children will find that these peanut butter versions are just as much fun to decorate with frosting, sprinkles and a dash of Yuletide imagination.

      1 cup creamy peanut butter
  3/4 cup sugar
  3/4 cup packed brown sugar
      2 eggs
  1/3 cup milk
      1 teaspoon vanilla extract
2-1/2 cups all-purpose flour
  1/2 teaspoon baking powder
  1/2 teaspoon baking soda
Vanilla frosting
Red, green, yellow and blue gel food coloring
Assorted colored sprinkles

In a large mixing bowl, cream peanut butter and sugars. Beat in the eggs, milk and vanilla. Combine the flour, baking powder and baking soda; add to creamed mixture and mix well. Cover and refrigerate for 2 hours or until easy to handle.

On a lightly floured surface, roll out dough to 1/4-in. thickness. Cut with 2-in. to 4-in. cookie cutters. Place 2 in. apart on ungreased baking sheets. Bake at 375° for 7-9 minutes or until edges are browned. Cool for 1 minute before removing from pans to wire racks to cool completely. Frost and decorate as desired. **Yield:** about 4-1/2 dozen.

RASPBERRY NUT PINWHEELS
Pat Habiger, Spearville, Kansas
(Pictured on page 41)

I won first prize in a recipe contest with these yummy swirl cookies. The taste of raspberry and walnuts really comes through and they're so much fun to make!

  1/2 cup butter (no substitutes), softened
      1 cup sugar
      1 egg
      1 teaspoon vanilla extract
      2 cups all-purpose flour
      1 teaspoon baking powder
  1/4 cup seedless raspberry jam
  3/4 cup finely chopped walnuts

In a mixing bowl, cream butter and sugar. Beat in egg and vanilla. Combine the flour and baking powder; gradually add to creamed mixture. Roll out dough between waxed paper into a 12-in. square. Remove top piece of waxed paper. Spread dough with jam and sprinkle with nuts. Roll up tightly jelly-roll style, starting with a long side; wrap in plastic wrap. Refrigerate for 2 hours or until firm.

Unwrap dough and cut into 1/4-in. slices. Place 2 in. apart on ungreased baking sheets. Bake at 375° for 9-12 minutes or until edges are lightly browned. Remove to wire racks to cool. **Yield:** about 3-1/2 dozen.

CHOCOLATE-DRIZZLED CHERRY BARS
Janice Heikkila, Deer Creek, Minnesota
(Pictured on page 41)

I've been making bars since I was in third grade, but these are special. I bake them for the church Christmas party every year…and folks always rave about them and ask for a copy of the recipe.

      2 cups all-purpose flour
      2 cups quick-cooking oats
1-1/2 cups sugar
1-1/4 cups butter *or* margarine, softened
      1 can (21 ounces) cherry pie filling
      1 teaspoon almond extract
  1/4 cup semisweet chocolate chips
  3/4 teaspoon shortening

In a mixing bowl, combine flour, oats, sugar and butter until crumbly. Set aside 1-1/2 cups for topping. Press remaining crumb mixture into an ungreased 13-in. x 9-in. x 2-in. baking dish. Bake at 350° for 15-18 minutes or until edges begin to brown.

In a bowl, combine pie filling and extract; carefully spread over crust. Sprinkle with reserved crumb mixture. Bake 20-25 minutes longer or until edges and topping are lightly browned. In a microwave or heavy saucepan, melt chocolate chips and shortening; stir until smooth. Drizzle over warm bars. Cool completely on a wire rack. **Yield:** 3 dozen.

CHOCOLATE MINT CREAMS
Beverly Fehner, Gladstone, Missouri
(Pictured on page 41)

This recipe came from an old family friend and is always high on everyone's cookie request list. I make at least six batches for Noel nibbling and give some away as gifts.

1 cup butter (no substitutes), softened
1-1/2 cups confectioners' sugar
2 squares (1 ounce *each*) unsweetened chocolate, melted and cooled
1 egg
1 teaspoon vanilla extract
2-1/2 cups all-purpose flour
1 teaspoon baking soda
1 teaspoon cream of tartar
1/4 teaspoon salt
FROSTING:
1/4 cup butter, softened
2 cups confectioners' sugar
2 tablespoons milk
1/2 teaspoon peppermint extract
Green food coloring, optional

In a large mixing bowl, cream butter and confectioners' sugar. Add the chocolate, egg and vanilla; mix well. Combine the dry ingredients; gradually add to creamed mixture, beating well. Shape dough into a 2-in.-diameter roll; wrap in plastic wrap. Refrigerate for 1 hour or until firm.

Unwrap dough and cut into 1/8-in. slices. Place 2 in. apart on ungreased baking sheets. Bake at 400° for 7-8 minutes or until edges are firm. Remove to wire racks to cool. In a small mixing bowl, combine frosting ingredients. Frost cookies. Store in airtight containers. **Yield:** about 6 dozen.

EGGNOG SNICKERDOODLES
Darlene Markel, Salem, Oregon

It simply wouldn't be Christmas without these melt-in-your-mouth cookies on my platter! They have a lovely eggnog flavor and look great with their crunchy tops. The aroma while they bake is as delectable as their taste.

1/2 cup butter (no substitutes), softened
1/2 cup shortening
1-3/4 cups sugar, *divided*
2 eggs
1/4 to 1/2 teaspoon rum extract
2-3/4 cups all-purpose flour
2 teaspoons cream of tartar
1 teaspoon baking soda
1/4 teaspoon salt
2 teaspoons ground nutmeg

In a mixing bowl, cream butter, shortening and 1-1/2 cups sugar. Beat in eggs and extract. Combine the flour, cream of tartar, baking soda and salt; gradually add to creamed mixture. In a shallow bowl, combine the nutmeg and remaining sugar. Roll dough into 1-in. balls; roll in sugar mixture. Place 2 in. apart on ungreased baking sheets. Bake at 400° for 10-12 minutes or until lightly browned. Remove to wire racks to cool. **Yield:** 6-1/2 dozen.

LEMON-LIME CRACKLE COOKIES
Ada Merwin, Waterford, Michigan

You can taste the spirit of Christmases past in these chewy old-time cookies with their crackled tops and lemony flavor. They're a luscious addition to cookie exchanges!

1/2 cup flaked coconut
2 teaspoons grated lemon peel
2 teaspoons grated lime peel
2 cups whipped topping
2 eggs
2 tablespoons dry whipped topping mix*
1 teaspoon lemon juice
1 package (18-1/4 ounces) lemon cake mix
Confectioners' sugar

In a blender or food processor, combine the coconut, lemon peel and lime peel. Cover and process until finely chopped, about 30 seconds; set aside. In a mixing bowl, combine whipped topping, eggs, dry whipped topping mix and lemon juice. Add dry cake mix and coconut mixture; mix well.

Drop by tablespoonfuls into a bowl of confectioners' sugar. Shape into balls. Place 2 in. apart on greased baking sheets. Bake at 350° for 10-12 minutes or until edges are golden brown. Remove to wire racks to cool. **Yield:** about 3 dozen.

*Editor's Note: This recipe was tested with Dream Whip topping.

BUTTERSCOTCH MERINGUE BARS
Betty Behnken, Beverly Hills, Florida

These fast and easy cookies are unlike any others I've eaten. They're irresistibly rich and always draw "oohs", "aahs" and requests for the recipe after the very first bite!

1 cup butter-flavored shortening
1/2 cup sugar
1/2 cup packed brown sugar
3 egg yolks
1 tablespoon water
3 teaspoons vanilla extract
2 cups all-purpose flour
1/4 teaspoon baking soda
1/4 teaspoon salt
1 cup butterscotch chips
MERINGUE:
3 egg whites
1 cup packed brown sugar
1 cup chopped walnuts

In a mixing bowl, cream shortening and sugars. Beat in egg yolks, water and vanilla. Combine the flour, baking soda and salt; gradually add to creamed mixture. Spread into a greased 13-in. x 9-in. x 2-in. baking pan. Sprinkle with butterscotch chips and pat lightly.

For meringue, in a small mixing bowl, beat egg whites until stiff peaks form. Gradually add brown sugar, beating well. Spread over chips. Sprinkle with walnuts and gently press into meringue. Bake at 350° for 25-30 minutes or until golden brown. Cool on a wire rack. Cut into bars. Refrigerate leftovers. **Yield:** 3 dozen.

DUTCH SPICE COOKIES
Mary Peterson, Charleston, Rhode Island

My sister gave me the recipe for these cookies, which have become a holiday tradition at our house. My kids tear into the spicy, crisp cookies right out of the oven. I prefer them cooled—but it's risky waiting. I might not get any!

    3/4 cup butter (no substitutes), softened
        1 cup packed brown sugar
2-1/4 cups all-purpose flour
        2 teaspoons ground cinnamon
    1/2 teaspoon ground mace
    1/2 teaspoon crushed aniseed
    1/4 teaspoon *each* ground ginger, nutmeg and
        cloves
    1/4 teaspoon baking powder
    1/8 teaspoon salt
        3 tablespoons milk
        1 cup finely chopped slivered almonds

In a mixing bowl, cream butter and brown sugar. Combine the flour, spices, baking powder and salt; gradually add to creamed mixture. Stir in milk and almonds. Roll dough into a 16-in. x 10-in. rectangle between two sheets of waxed paper. Cut into 2-in. squares. Cover with waxed paper and refrigerate for 30 minutes.

Place squares 1 in. apart on ungreased baking sheets. Bake at 375° for 8-10 minutes or until firm. Remove to wire racks to cool. **Yield:** 40 cookies.

APRICOT CREAM CHEESE DROPS
Melinda Leonowitz, Birdsboro, Pennsylvania

This treasured recipe is from a favorite aunt. Her soft, rich cookies have a yummy apricot flavor, but you could substitute strawberry, pineapple or raspberry preserves if you prefer.

    1/2 cup butter (no substitutes), softened
        1 package (3 ounces) cream cheese, softened
    1/2 cup apricot preserves
    1/4 cup packed brown sugar
        1 tablespoon milk
1-1/4 cups all-purpose flour
1-1/2 teaspoons baking powder
1-1/2 teaspoons ground cinnamon
    1/4 teaspoon salt
FROSTING:
        1 cup confectioners' sugar
    1/4 cup apricot preserves
        1 tablespoon butter, softened
        1 to 2 teaspoons milk
Ground nuts *or* flaked coconut

In a mixing bowl, cream the butter, cream cheese, apricot preserves, brown sugar and milk. Combine the flour, baking powder, cinnamon and salt; gradually add to creamed mixture. Drop by teaspoonfuls onto ungreased baking sheets. Bake at 350° for 8-10 minutes or until lightly browned. Remove to wire racks to cool.

For frosting, in a bowl, combine the confectioners' sugar, apricot preserves, butter and enough milk to achieve desired consistency. Frost cookies. Sprinkle with nuts or coconut. **Yield:** 3 dozen.

CHERRY DATE COOKIES
Hope Huggins, Turlock, California

My mother made these festive drop cookies as far back as I can remember—80 years at least. We called them "the Christmas cookies", maybe because they're so full of fruit and nuts.

        1 cup shortening
1-1/2 cups packed brown sugar
        3 eggs
2-1/2 cups all-purpose flour
        1 teaspoon baking soda
        1 teaspoon ground cinnamon
    1/2 teaspoon salt
        3 tablespoons hot water
        1 cup chopped walnuts
    1/2 cup chopped dates
    1/2 cup quartered maraschino cherries

In a mixing bowl, cream shortening and brown sugar. Add eggs, one at a time, beating well after each addition. Combine the flour, baking soda, cinnamon and salt; add to creamed mixture alternately with water. Stir in walnuts, dates and cherries. Drop by rounded teaspoonfuls 2 in. apart onto ungreased baking sheets. Bake at 375° for 8-9 minutes or until golden brown. Remove to wire racks to cool. **Yield:** 10-1/2 dozen.

Editor's Note: To make 5 dozen larger cookies, drop dough by rounded tablespoonfuls 3 in. apart onto ungreased baking sheets. Bake for 9-10 minutes.

TRIPLE LAYERED BARS
Sarah Nut, Rachel Wallace, Maranda Abercrombie
Little Rock, Arkansas

We created these chocolaty bars in our food science class at school. They're really pretty drizzled in white and taste great!

        1 cup butter (no substitutes), softened
        1 cup sugar
        1 egg
    1/4 teaspoon lemon extract
        2 cups all-purpose flour
FILLING:
    1/2 cup butter, cubed
        2 squares (1 ounce *each*) unsweetened chocolate
        2 eggs
        1 cup sugar
        1 teaspoon vanilla extract
    1/2 cup all-purpose flour
    1/2 teaspoon salt
        4 ounces white candy coating, melted

In a large mixing bowl, cream butter and sugar. Beat in egg and lemon extract. Gradually add the flour. Press into a greased 15-in. x 10-in. x 1-in. baking pan; set aside. In a heavy saucepan, melt butter and chocolate until smooth. Remove from the heat; cool slightly. In a mixing bowl, beat eggs, sugar and vanilla. Beat in cooled chocolate mixture, flour and salt. Pour over the crust.

Bake at 350° for 20-22 minutes or until a toothpick inserted near the center comes out clean. Cool completely on a wire rack. Drizzle candy coating over bars. Cool for 20 minutes before cutting. **Yield:** 32 bars.

MOLASSES SUGAR COOKIES
Kay Curtis, Guthrie, Oklahoma
(Pictured at right)

There's nothing really fancy about these cookies, but they're my husband's all-time favorite. He enjoys their chewy, comforting flavor and the childhood memories they bring back.

   3/4 cup vegetable oil
     1 cup sugar
   1/4 cup molasses
     1 egg
     2 cups all-purpose flour
     2 teaspoons baking soda
     1 teaspoon ground cinnamon
   1/2 teaspoon salt
   1/2 teaspoon ground cloves
   1/2 teaspoon ground ginger
Additional sugar

In a large mixing bowl, combine the oil, sugar and molasses. Add egg; mix well. Combine the flour, baking soda, cinnamon, salt, cloves and ginger; add to sugar mixture and mix well. Cover and refrigerate for 4 hours or until easy to handle.

   Shape dough into 1-in. balls; roll in sugar. Place 3 in. apart on greased baking sheets. Bake at 375° for 7-9 minutes or until tops are cracked and edges are set. Cool for 2-3 minutes before removing from pans to wire racks. **Yield:** about 4 dozen.

RASPBERRY MERINGUES
Iola Egle, McCook, Nebraska

As rosy pink as Santa's cheeks, these merry meringue cookies are drizzled with dark chocolate and almost too pretty to eat. Pecans add a nice crunch to these chewy treats. They lend a "berry" festive touch to my Christmas cookie tray.

     3 egg whites
     3 tablespoons plus 1 teaspoon raspberry gelatin
       powder
   3/4 cup sugar
     1 teaspoon white vinegar
   1/8 teaspoon salt
     2 cups (12 ounces) semisweet chocolate chips
   1/2 cup finely chopped pecans
TOPPING:
   1/4 cup semisweet chocolate chips
     1 teaspoon shortening

Place egg whites in a small mixing bowl; let stand at room temperature for 30 minutes. Beat egg whites until soft peaks form. Gradually add gelatin, beating until combined. Gradually add sugar, 1 tablespoon at a time, beating until stiff peaks form. Beat in vinegar and salt. Fold in chocolate chips and nuts.

   Drop by rounded teaspoonfuls onto parchment-lined baking sheets. Bake at 250° for 20-25 minutes or until firm to the touch. Turn oven off; leave cookies in the oven with door ajar for about 1-1/2 hours or until cool. In a microwave or heavy saucepan, melt chocolate chips and shortening; stir until smooth. Drizzle over cookies. **Yield:** 7-1/2 dozen.

CHOCOLATE MINT CRISPS
Karen Bland, Gove, Kansas

If you like chocolate and mint, you can't help but love these delicious crispy cookies with their creamy icing. We always make them for the holidays…and guests can never seem to eat just one!

1-1/2 cups packed brown sugar
   3/4 cup butter *or* margarine, cubed
     2 tablespoons plus 1-1/2 teaspoons water
     2 cups (12 ounces) semisweet chocolate chips
     2 eggs
2-1/2 cups all-purpose flour
1-1/4 teaspoons baking soda
   1/2 teaspoon salt
     3 packages (4.67 ounces *each*) mint Andes candies

In a heavy saucepan, combine the brown sugar, butter and water. Cook and stir over low heat until butter is melted and mixture is smooth. Remove from the heat; stir in chocolate chips until melted. Transfer to a mixing bowl. Let stand for 10 minutes. With mixer on high speed, add eggs one at a time, beating well after each addition. Combine the flour, baking soda and salt; add to chocolate mixture, beating on low until blended. Cover and refrigerate for 8 hours or overnight.

   Roll dough into 1-in. balls. Place 3 in. apart on lightly greased baking sheets. Bake at 350° for 11-13 minutes or until edges are set and tops are puffed and cracked (cookies will become crisp after cooling). Immediately top each cookie with a mint. Let stand for 1-2 minutes; spread over cookie. Remove to wire racks; let stand until chocolate is set and cookies are cooled. **Yield:** about 6-1/2 dozen.

Dazzling Desserts

Top off your gala holiday meals and buffets with one or more of these fabulous festive desserts. Guests will carol your praises and come back for seconds!

PLUM ICE CREAM
Jo Baker, Litchfield, Illinois
(Pictured on page 46)

Here's a pretty ice cream that is such a light refreshing finale to a holiday meal, it melts any resistance to dessert!

2 cans (30 ounces *each*) whole plums
6 cups milk
4 cups whipping cream
2 cups sugar
1/3 cup lemon juice
Red food coloring, optional

Drain plums, reserving 1 cup syrup. Peel plums and remove pits. In a food processor or blender, cover and process plums until smooth. In a bowl, combine the milk, cream, sugar, lemon juice, plums, reserved syrup and food coloring if desired. Stir until sugar is dissolved.

Fill cylinder of ice cream freezer two-thirds full; freeze according to manufacturer's directions. Refrigerate remaining mixture until ready to freeze. Allow to ripen in ice cream freezer or firm up in refrigerator freezer for 2-4 hours before serving. **Yield:** 4 quarts.

CARAMEL PECAN CHEESECAKE
Deidre Sizer, Kettering, Ohio
(Pictured on page 46)

I created this creamy cheesecake using two favorites—caramel and pecans. It's a stunning cake and rivals any I've tasted.

2 cups crushed shortbread cookies
3 tablespoons butter *or* margarine, melted
1/4 cup plus 2 tablespoons all-purpose flour, *divided*
1 jar (12-1/4 ounces) caramel ice cream topping
1 cup chopped pecans
5 packages (8 ounces *each*) cream cheese, softened
1-3/4 cups sugar
1-1/2 teaspoons vanilla extract
4 eggs
2 egg yolks
1/3 cup whipping cream
SOUR CREAM TOPPING:
2 cups (16 ounces) sour cream
1/3 cup sugar

In a bowl, combine cookie crumbs and butter; mix well. Press onto the bottom and 1 in. up the sides of a greased 10-in. springform pan. Place pan on a baking sheet. Bake at 350° for 8-10 minutes or until set. Cool on a wire rack.

In a small bowl, stir 1/4 cup flour into the caramel topping. Set aside 1/3 cup caramel mixture and 2 tablespoons

pecans for garnish. Drizzle remaining caramel mixture over crust; sprinkle with remaining pecans. In a mixing bowl, beat the cream cheese, sugar, vanilla and remaining flour until smooth. Add eggs and yolks; beat on low speed just until combined. Stir in cream. Pour over crust. Bake at 325° for 65-70 minutes or until center is almost set.

Combine sour cream and sugar; carefully spread over warm filling. Bake 10-12 minutes longer or until topping is set. Cool on a wire rack for 10 minutes. Carefully run a knife around edge of pan to loosen; cool 1 hour longer. Chill for 8 hours or overnight. Remove sides of pan. Just before serving, drizzle with reserved caramel mixture and sprinkle with reserved pecans. Refrigerate leftovers. **Yield:** 12 servings.

ICE CREAM TUNNEL CAKE
Holly Jean VeDepo, West Liberty, Iowa
(Pictured on page 46)

My son found this yummy recipe a few years ago and now it's a Yuletide tradition. A boxed mix makes preparation easy. For a fun variation, try mint-chocolate chip ice cream.

1 package (18-1/4 ounces) chocolate cake mix
1 quart vanilla ice cream, slightly softened
1/2 cup mint chocolate chips*
1/2 cup light corn syrup
1 tablespoon whipping cream
1/2 teaspoon vanilla extract

Prepare cake mix according to package directions. Pour batter into a greased and floured 10-in. fluted tube pan. Bake at 350° for 35-40 minutes or until a toothpick inserted near the center comes out clean. Cool for 10 minutes before removing from pan to a wire rack. Cool completely.

Slice top fourth off cake; set aside. Using a sharp knife, carefully hollow out bottom, leaving a 1-in. shell (save removed cake for another use). Place cake shell in freezer for 1 hour. Fill tunnel with ice cream; replace cake top. Cover and freeze for at least 6 hours.

Just before serving, melt chips and corn syrup in a microwave; stir until smooth. Stir in cream and vanilla. Spoon over cake. **Yield:** 12 servings.

***Editor's Note:** If mint chocolate chips are not available, place 1/2 cup semisweet chocolate chips and a few drops of peppermint extract in a plastic bag; seal and toss to coat. Let stand for 24-48 hours before using.

● Some desserts are elegant enough to make an impressive centerpiece for a holiday buffet table all by themselves! Other options might include a selection of special cheeses, fruits or chocolates to be served after dinner and trimmed with sprays of greens, bright bows or glass ornaments.

DELECTABLE HOLIDAY DESSERTS. Almost too pretty to eat, these luscious treats include Ice Cream Tunnel Cake, Plum Ice Cream and Caramel Pecan Cheesecake (p. 47, clockwise from top).

CRANBERRY-PEAR APPLE CRISP
Louis Gelzer, Oak Bluffs, Massachusetts

With its crunchy golden topping and flavorful blend of tart cranberries and sweet apples and pears, this dessert makes a refreshing finish to heavy winter meals.

    8 medium pears, peeled and sliced
    4 medium tart apples, peeled and sliced
    2 cups fresh *or* frozen cranberries, thawed
    1 cup sugar
    3/4 cup all-purpose flour
TOPPING:
    1 cup packed brown sugar
    3/4 cup all-purpose flour
    3/4 cup quick-cooking oats
    1/4 teaspoon ground cinnamon
    1/2 cup cold butter *or* margarine

In a large bowl, toss the fruit, sugar and flour. Pour into a greased 13-in. x 9-in. x 2-in. baking dish. For topping, in a bowl, combine the brown sugar, flour, oats and cinnamon. Cut in butter until mixture resembles coarse crumbs. Sprinkle over fruit mixture. Bake at 350° for 60-65 minutes or until fruit is tender and topping is golden brown. **Yield:** 12-14 servings.

ORANGE MOUSSE CHOCOLATE TORTE
Vicky Monk, Citrus Heights, California

I always get compliments from the chocolate lovers at my table when I serve them this cool tangy torte with its rich flourless chocolate cake.

    1 cup butter (no substitutes), cubed
    9 squares (1 ounce *each*) bittersweet chocolate, chopped
    3/4 cup sugar
    1/2 cup ground hazelnuts, toasted
    4 eggs
MOUSSE:
    1 cup orange juice concentrate
    1/3 cup sugar
    1/3 cup water
    1 envelope unflavored gelatin
    3 tablespoons lemon juice
    14 squares (1 ounce *each*) white baking chocolate, chopped
    1/3 cup sour cream
    2 cups whipping cream
White chocolate curls and baking cocoa, optional

In a heavy saucepan, melt butter and bittersweet chocolate over low heat, stirring constantly until smooth. Remove from the heat; whisk in sugar and nuts. Add eggs, one at a time, until blended. Pour into a greased 9-in. springform pan. Place pan on a baking sheet. Bake at 325° for 45 minutes or until a toothpick inserted near the center comes out with moist crumbs. Cool on a wire rack. Refrigerate.

For mousse, in a saucepan, heat the orange juice concentrate, sugar and water until warm. In a small bowl, sprinkle gelatin over lemon juice; let stand for 1 minute. Add to orange mixture; stir until gelatin is dissolved. Add white chocolate; stir just until melted. Whisk in sour cream. Pour into a large bowl. Refrigerate, stirring often, until cool and thickened but not set, about 1-1/2 hours.

In a small mixing bowl, beat cream until stiff peaks form; fold into orange mixture. Pour over crust (pan will be full). Refrigerate for several hours or overnight. Carefully run a knife around edge of pan to loosen; remove torte from pan. Garnish with chocolate curls and cocoa if desired. **Yield:** 12-15 servings.

    Editor's Note: This recipe does not use flour.

FROZEN CRANBERRY CUPS
Marilyn Huntley, St. Augustine, Florida

It's just not Christmas at our house without this lighter-than-air whipped dessert. It couldn't be easier to make…and looks so festive in foil cups. Guests always ask for the recipe.

    3/4 cup whole-berry cranberry sauce
    3 tablespoons orange juice concentrate
    2 tablespoons chopped pecans
    1/2 cup whipping cream
    2 tablespoons sugar

Place the cranberry sauce in a bowl; chop the cranberries. Stir in the orange juice concentrate and pecans; set aside. In a mixing bowl, beat cream until soft peaks form. Gradually add sugar, beating until stiff peaks form. Fold into the cranberry mixture. Fill foil-lined muffin cups two-thirds full. Cover and freeze until firm. Remove from the freezer 15 minutes before serving. **Yield:** 8 servings.

PECAN POUND CAKE
Joan Ferguson, Elkhorn, Nebraska

This tender cake has been a family favorite for years. Chock-full of nuts, it has a rich buttery taste, a crispy crust—and makes a wonderful substitute for fruitcake at Christmas! Delicious with coffee or tea, this cake also freezes very well.

    2 cups butter (no substitutes), softened
    2 cups sugar
    9 eggs
    1 tablespoon lemon juice
    3 teaspoons vanilla extract
    1 teaspoon grated lemon peel
    3 cups all-purpose flour
    1 teaspoon baking powder
    1/4 teaspoon salt
    4 cups chopped pecans
1-1/2 cups golden raisins
Confectioners' sugar, optional

In a large mixing bowl, cream butter and sugar. Add eggs, one at a time, beating well after each addition. Beat in the lemon juice, vanilla and lemon peel. Combine the flour, baking powder and salt; gradually add to creamed mixture. Fold in pecans and raisins.

Pour into a greased 10-in. fluted tube pan. Bake at 350° for 1-1/4 to 1-1/2 hours or until a toothpick inserted near the center comes out clean. Cool for 10 minutes; remove from pan to a wire rack to cool completely. Dust with confectioners' sugar if desired. **Yield:** 12-16 servings.

ORANGE LAYER CAKE
Virginia Ford, El Sobrante, California

My sister gave me this recipe over 50 years ago...and I still make it for Christmas. With its creamy nut frosting and tangy orange flavor, it's a family favorite.

      1/2 cup shortening
1-1/2 cups sugar
      2 eggs
      1 tablespoon grated orange peel
2-1/4 cups all-purpose flour
      2 teaspoons baking powder
      1 teaspoon salt
      1/4 teaspoon baking soda
      3/4 cup water
      1/4 cup orange juice
FILLING/FROSTING:
      2 tablespoons plus 1-1/2 teaspoons all-purpose
         flour
      1/2 cup milk
      1/2 cup shortening
      1/2 cup sugar
      1/4 teaspoon salt
      1/2 teaspoon vanilla extract
      1/2 cup chopped walnuts
      1 cup confectioners' sugar

In a mixing bowl, cream shortening and sugar. Add eggs, one at a time, beating well after each addition. Beat in orange peel. Combine the flour, baking powder, salt and baking soda; add to creamed mixture alternately with water and orange juice. Pour into two greased and floured 9-in. round baking pans. Bake at 350° for 20-25 minutes or until a toothpick comes out clean. Cool for 10 minutes before removing from pans to wire racks to cool completely.

In a saucepan, stir flour and milk until smooth. Bring to a boil; cook and stir for 1 minute or until thickened. Remove from the heat; cool to lukewarm. In a mixing bowl, beat shortening, sugar and salt. Add vanilla; mix well. Add cooled milk mixture; beat on high speed for 5 minutes or until fluffy. Remove about 2/3 cup; fold in nuts. Spread between cake layers. To the remaining filling, add confectioners' sugar; beat until light and fluffy. Frost top and sides of cake. **Yield:** 12 servings.

CHERRY ALMOND PIE
Johanna Gerow, Raytown, Missouri

I love trying new recipes for Christmas, but my husband can't get enough of traditional classics—like this cherry pie.

      2 cans (14 ounces *each*) pitted tart cherries
      1 cup sugar
      1/4 cup cornstarch
      1/8 teaspoon salt
      2 tablespoons butter *or* margarine
      1/2 teaspoon almond extract
      1/2 teaspoon vanilla extract
      1/4 teaspoon red food coloring, optional
Pastry for double-crust pie (9 inches)
      1 egg yolk, beaten
Additional sugar

Drain cherries, reserving 1 cup juice. In a saucepan, com-bine the sugar, cornstarch and salt; gradually stir in reserved cherry juice until smooth. Bring to a boil; cook and stir for 2 minutes or until thickened. Remove from the heat; stir in butter, extracts and food coloring if desired. Fold in cherries. Cool slightly.

Line a 9-in. pie plate with bottom crust; trim pastry to 1 in. beyond edge of plate. Pour filling into crust. Roll out remaining pastry; make a lattice crust. Trim, seal and flute edges. Brush lattice top with egg yolk. Sprinkle with additional sugar. Cover edges loosely with foil. Bake at 425° for 15 minutes. Remove foil. Bake 20-25 minutes longer or until crust is golden brown and filling is bubbly. Cool on a wire rack. **Yield:** 6-8 servings.

JEWELED SHERBET MOLD
Mary Gaylord, Balsam Lake, Wisconsin

Besides being a colorful addition to any holiday buffet, this dessert keeps well and is deliciously different.

      1 pint lime sherbet, softened
      1 pint lemon sherbet, softened
      1 can (8 ounces) crushed pineapple, drained
      1/3 cup chopped mixed candied fruit
      1/4 teaspoon rum extract, optional
Whipped cream and maraschino cherries, optional

Line a 1-1/2-qt. metal or glass bowl with plastic wrap or foil. Pack lime sherbet into the bottom of the bowl; smooth top. Freeze for 15 minutes. In another bowl, combine lemon sherbet, pineapple, candied fruit and extract if desired. Spoon over lime sherbet; smooth top. Cover and freeze for 2 hours or until firm.

Remove from the freezer 15 minutes before serving. Uncover and invert onto a round serving platter. Remove bowl and plastic wrap; smooth sides. Garnish with whipped cream and cherries if desired. **Yield:** 12-14 servings.

STRAWBERRY DESSERT
Delores Romyn, Stratton, Ontario

I like to garnish this dessert with strawberry slices arranged to look like poinsettias—it's pretty, festive and feeds a crowd!

      1 package (3 ounces) ladyfingers, split
      1 package (4-3/4 ounces) strawberry Junket
         Danish Dessert*
1-3/4 cups cold water
      2 pints fresh strawberries, sliced
      1 carton (8 ounces) frozen whipped topping,
         thawed
Additional sliced strawberries, optional

Place ladyfingers in a single layer in a 13-in. x 9-in. x 2-in. dish; set aside. In a saucepan, bring dessert mix and water to a boil. Cook and stir for 1 minute. Cool for 4-5 minutes; fold in strawberries. Spoon over ladyfingers; spread gently. Cover and refrigerate for 3-4 hours. Spread with whipped topping. Garnish with additional strawberries if desired. **Yield:** 12-15 servings.

*Editor's Note: Junket Danish Dessert can be found in the pudding section of most grocery stores.

Fancy-Full Food

Sweet Crafted Treat Holds Berry Merry Wishes

FRIENDS AND FAMILY won't be able to "contain" themselves when you present this Christmas masterpiece.

It's twice the treat, since your guests can eat both the elegant container handcrafted from chocolate, as well as the juicy chocolate-dipped strawberries piled high inside.

Our *CW* kitchen crew came up with this beautifully festive confection, guaranteed to draw oohs and aahs of approval. And they have included all the directions and tips you will need to duplicate this delicacy!

For added color contrast, try dipping whole dried apricots as well as strawberries in the chocolate.

FRUIT-FILLED CHOCOLATE CONTAINER

- 16 squares (1 ounce *each*) semisweet chocolate
- 2 tablespoons shortening
- 2-1/2 ounces white candy coating
- 1 tablespoon light corn syrup
- **CHOCOLATE-DIPPED BERRIES:**
- 24 squares (1 ounce *each*) semisweet chocolate
- 5 teaspoons shortening
- 1-1/2 teaspoons almond extract
- 5 dozen large fresh strawberries (about 2-1/2 quarts)

Line a 9-in. round baking pan with aluminum foil; set aside. In a heavy saucepan over low heat, melt chocolate and shortening; stir until smooth. Pour 3/4 cup into prepared pan; chill for 10 minutes or until firm. Spread a thin coating of the remaining melted chocolate around sides of pan (see photo 1); chill for 5 minutes. Continue coating until all of the melted chocolate has been used.

Break white candy coating into chunks; place in a microwave-safe bowl. Microwave at 70% power for 1 minute; stir. Microwave in 10-second intervals or until melted; stir until smooth. Add corn syrup; stir until mixture is thick. Pour onto waxed paper; press to 1/2-in. thickness. Let stand for 15-20 minutes or until easy to handle. Set aside 1 teaspoon for assembly.

Divide remaining coating into six equal portions. Roll each into a 15-in. rope. Press three rope ends together; braid and press end to secure. Repeat with remaining ropes. Set aside both braids.

For Chocolate-Dipped Berries: Melt chocolate and shortening in a microwave or heavy saucepan. Stir in almond extract. Dip strawberries halfway, allowing excess to drip off. Place on a waxed paper-lined tray; refrigerate for 30 minutes or until set.

To assemble, carefully remove chocolate container from pan by slowly pulling up on foil lining (see photo 2). Peel foil to remove.

Place small dabs of reserved white coating around top edge of container to secure the braids (see photo 3). Press one braid around half of container. Repeat with other braid; trim to fit if necessary. Cover and refrigerate until serving. Fill with chocolate-dipped berries. **Yield:** 1 chocolate container and about 2-1/2 dozen berries.

Photo 1. Using a small spatula, spread a thin even coat of the remaining chocolate around the sides of pan. Chill for 5 minutes. Repeat until there is no more chocolate remaining.

Photo 2. Carefully remove your chocolate container from the pan, using the foil lining to lift it out. Invert container carefully onto a flat surface. Then gently peel off the foil.

Candy-Coated Tips for Trimming

- To add a special Christmas touch to this chocolate container, melt a little extra white candy coating. Divide into two equal portions, adding red paste or gel food coloring to one portion and green to the other. Roll coating to 1/4-inch thickness and cut with 1-inch cookie cutters into shapes such as holly leaves and berries or snowflakes. Attach cutout shapes to sides of container with a dab of melted chocolate.
- To give your strawberries an extra-festive look, crush some red and green hard mint candies. After dipping berries in melted chocolate, roll in the crushed candies and place on waxed paper until dry. Or drizzle a little melted white candy coating in fun patterns over the chocolate-dipped end of each fruit.

Photo 3. Place small dollops of the reserved coating mixture around the top edge of container. Carefully place the braid around the same edge and press down gently to secure.

Her House Is a Treasure Trove Of Merry Christmas Keepsakes

FROM STOCKINGS hung by the chimney with care to halls decked with holly—and a whole sleighful of details in between—Patricia Nolan pulls out all the stops when decorating her 1874 farmhouse for the holidays.

"I was raised in a house where Christmas meant more than anything in the world," she says with a smile.

And it's clear, even from the garland-draped fence and front door to her Hustisford, Wisconsin home, that Patricia is carrying on that same festive tradition.

Holiday collectibles, many of them antiques, are tucked into every nook and cranny, among the warm Victorian and country furnishings in every room.

At 80, Patricia has spent the last 35 years collecting old-fashioned ornaments, Santas, snowmen and other seasonal trims that add a rich nostalgic note—and a wealth of stories—to every room's Yuletide decor.

"It wasn't until I got a little older that I started appreciating things from my grandma's house and began inheriting a few things that had great sentimental value to me," she explains.

Merry Mantel

Today, those treasures are tucked on mantels, grouped on shelves and sills, or hung on the tall, glittering tree that dominates her living room and boasts close to 500 ornaments!

"The oldest one dates from shortly after 1900. It's a little swan with a cradle on its back holding Baby Jesus," she notes.

"But my favorite is that big German angel that's almost as big as a doll." She points to a winged, wax-covered composition figure with blond curly hair, a

GAY GARLANDS, wonderful memories and aromas and festive Yuletide trims "all through the house" welcome visitors to the historic Wisconsin home of Patricia Nolan (below).

piece of rabbit fur across her torso and a wand in her hand.

"My mother bought that when I was little, and it was always on our tree for as far back as I can remember. It reminds me of my mother."

Beside the tree, garlands of greens with red berries drape her fireplace and even top the painting above it. Her mantel is merry with a shiny brass sleigh and reindeer, a quartet of tiny snowmen and some of her many Santa figures.

There's an antique fellow in dark-red velvet, a whimsical St. Nick balance toy, a dangling folk-art elf and the jolly

Photos: Jack Long/LongShots

PRESENTS 'NEATH THE TREE, boughs of evergreens framing a fire's warm glow and a lifetime of treasured antique accents fill every corner of this room—and home. "Organization is the key," says Patricia, who decorates every inch—inside and out—herself. "It doesn't take long if you have a system." Below, a colorful cluster of her Byers' Choice carolers sing out the season's greetings and echo her own best wishes.

jumping-jack Santa she made herself.

"I can't come up with the ideas, but I can copy just about anything," she chuckles. "I guess you'd call me handy."

Her "hand" is evident everywhere in the lovely details that make this season—and Patricia's home—so bright. A stick snowman and teddy, bundled in winter wraps, warm themselves at the hearth…and even a wood duck decoy sports a cheery red hat!

Whimsical Trims

Holly sprigs trim every candlestick and sconce and tie back the drapes at wreathed windows. Bright Christmas pillows and throws nestle on couches and chairs, and miniature versions of gift-wrapped presents under the tree spill over to fill a fireside wicker sleigh.

Across the hall, her small parlor-like "red room" holds a hutch full of Patricia's many Christmas plates, her small Japanese stick Santas with clay faces (eight of them dating back to 1910), and six ancient "putz" sheep used in Moravian village and manger

scenes now grazing on her top shelf.

On a nearby tabletop, a group of handcrafted Byers' Choice collectibles gather 'round a lamppost (and more holly), recalling the story of Scrooge and the spirit of Christmases past.

"There really wasn't a lot of holiday

hoopdy-do when I was growing up," Patricia remembers. "Mother had a couple of chenille poinsettias and wreaths she brought out. That, and the tree, were all we had for decorations. But she baked fruitcakes and a ton of old-fashioned German spice cookies." ♂

In fact, follow the evergreen garlands downstairs to the kitchen, and you'll see some of her mother's tin cookie cutters, along with more Santas and snowmen…and a whole village of the little paper "glitter houses" people slipped over Christmas-tree bulbs decades ago.

Floor to ceiling, front door to back, Patricia's house is wrapped in Christmas keepsakes and the merry memories that make them precious.

It takes about a week to do the whole job herself but, just like the season itself, she says, "It keeps me young!" ✻

AGE-OLD ORNAMENTS on Patricia's tree and jolly holiday collectibles on shelves and sills celebrate the spirit of Christmases long ago. Below, prized paper "glitter houses" beckon beside her home's original back door.

Missouri Artist Gets Wired Up for Christmas

TWO WEATHERED screen doors opened a whole new world of possibilities for artist Dodie Eisenhauer from Daisy, Missouri.

Although the old doors didn't work as display space for her painted crafts as she had hoped, they prompted a new art form.

"I'd never seen anything but a fly swatter made out of screen wire," Dodie explains. "But when I needed to make a bow one morning, I remembered the unused screening I had purchased to fix up the doors and went to work."

Her "screen test" was such a success that Dodie also fashioned a fan, a basket and another bow and then painted them all.

"I took the samples to a wholesale show in Dallas and came home with a stack of orders," she recalls.

Now Dodie buys 100-foot rolls of screen wire to sculpt intricate angels, trees, poinsettias, tree-toppers, bowls, crosses and more.

"Angels are my biggest sellers, so I try to introduce a new version each year. They range in size from 3 inches to 5 feet," she notes.

"Sometimes design ideas come to me from playing with a piece of wire mesh. Other times, I have something in mind and sketch it first.

"Then I cut pieces of screen wire and 'hem' them so there are no sharp edges. After bending and shaping the wire the way I want, I use an air compressor/

paint gun to spray-paint each item. It's a challenge to keep the holes in the screen from clogging up!"

It's also a challenge to mold the abrasive wire without piercing the skin. "My daughter once complained about the wire mesh 'removing her fingerprints'," Dodie chuckles.

She and husband Bob, a rural postman, have five grown children—Jill, Jenny, Jadie, Tim and Aaron—who pitch in when they can. "Even my dad, who's 94, coils wire for small items and makes all the halos for my angels."

Before she became enmeshed in screen wire, Dodie brushed up rusty tinware she found at auctions. "I painted old bread boxes, kitchen scales and

kerosene heaters with flowers and fruit."

Now Dodie sells her wire creations at some 2,000 stores in the United States and Canada as well as at a few local craft shows.

The real satisfaction, though, comes at Christmastime. "Every year, I loan three life-size angels to a local church to suspend from the ceiling," she says. "It's been my greatest joy to see my wire angels helping to tell the story of Christmas."

Editor's Note: Dodie's shop, Village Designs at Grandma's House, is open from mid-November to December 31 and by appointment at 310 State Highway AA in Daisy, Missouri. Call toll-free at 1-800/268-3642 or log on to *www.villagedesigns.com*. ✱

WIREWORK. Creating intricate designs from abrasive screen wire can be a painstaking process. But it's one Dodie Eisenhauer, at right, has mastered. Her delicate-looking bows, trees, angels, florals and more have become so popular that Dodie has had to hire extra help to meet her holiday demands.

Photos: Charles Hutchings

The Christmas Coat

By Kathleen B. Dunkley of Lakewood, Colorado

THE WINTER of 1917, I remember severe blizzards battered our small town at the foot of the Rocky Mountains. Snow almost covered the windows of our house, and the door had to be forced open just to dig deep trails to the most important places—the outhouse, the well, the chicken coop, barn and woodshed.

Even the Christmas break from school seemed special that year because my father and two older brothers spent so much time indoors. Usually, they were occupied with outdoor chores.

And since there was no electricity to power the amusements of today—no telephones, computers or electronic games—we had to invent activities to occupy our time.

One day, my father filled a large pan with snow, brought it inside and mixed it with rich cream flavored with sugar and vanilla. We sat shivering around our pot-bellied stove as we enjoyed that delicious "snow ice cream", and wished we could think of a way to save some for hot summer days!

Wish Book

Christmas dreams centered mostly around the mail-order catalog that we thumbed through daily. We knew most of the items were only to be wished for, but that year, my parents actually selected a coat for me.

Oh, the picture was so beautiful! I remember I could hardly believe my good fortune or stand the wait.

On the day we had calculated the coat should arrive, my brother put on his warm mackinaw and high-buckled galoshes and waded through hip-deep snow all the way to the post office to get the coat.

When he finally came through our door with that parcel, I was nearly dancing with excitement! I'll never forget the wonderful aroma that came from that box...a big-city smell that was completely new to my country nose.

Mail Call

Inside, there was the long-awaited velvet coat with plush collar and cuffs. There was also a warm bonnet with pink ribbons and three small dogs' heads with glass eyes, *and* a soft, warm muff. Oh, it was delightful!

As I paraded around in my finery for the family, even Mama, who was ill, clapped her hands and said, "Just *look* at Tattie in her beautiful coat!"

Some time later, we made a special train trip to Colorado Springs just to have my photo taken (that's me at left). But as thrilled and happy as I was with my new coat, the photographer caught no hint of a smile! It simply wasn't the custom in those days.

About 10 years later, things changed drastically. I was orphaned and faced some difficult and dark days. But the sweet memory of that beautiful Christmas coat and the warmth of my family's love remained with me always to give me comfort and such pleasure. ✻

Magical Memories

Let's dream awhile of Christmas
And days of long ago...
When a wreath lit up the window,
Reflecting light on snow.

There was a certain magic
That filled the wintry air...
And smiles on children's faces
Were seen most everywhere.

Let's dream again of distant bells,
The home that we remember,
With those we loved around the tree,
On His birthday in December.

—Marjorie Lundell
Casa Grande, Arizona

Well-Dressed Dolls Have Lots of Character

ALL DOLLED UP for the holidays! Jan Simpich (top right) and husband Bob have handcrafted dolls to recall every Christmas tale and tradition—from Bethlehem to the North Pole to Dickens' carolers. Collectors clamor for their heirloom-quality faces and fashions.

DOLLS delight many a child on Christmas morning, but it's grown-ups who eagerly search for Jan Simpich's dolls under the tree.

Jan and her husband, Bob, of Colorado Springs, Colorado, have been designing Simpich Character Dolls for 51 years. The handcrafted collectibles, from crotchety Scrooge and Old-World carolers to whimsical elves and precious Cloud Babies, feature meticulously sculpted faces and elaborate clothing.

"The dolls were born out of necessity," Jan recalls. "As struggling newlyweds, our first Christmas was financially lean, so we created our first dolls as gifts for our parents. Friends saw the dolls and asked us to make more."

As demand for the dolls grew, the creative couple enlisted the help of neighbors, relatives and friends to fashion the figures. This "extended family" of 70 some artisans now works above the couple's retail space in Old Colorado City, a quaint historic district of Colorado Springs.

"All the dolls are still designed by members of our family," Jan points out. "Bob and I sculpt most of the heads, working in clay to get details and facial expressions just right.

"Then a mold is made and the head is cast in gypsum cement or porcelain and hand-painted. Next, it's attached to a wire body, which is wrapped in cotton and shaped. Each character is dressed in a hand-sewn outfit and mounted on a base. I oversee the clothing on all the new pieces," Jan adds.

"Our oldest son, Ragan, has created some Western characters and Civil War soldiers. And our son David, a puppeteer, designed a few that resemble his marionettes."

The couple's four children and 10 grandchildren have also lent their names—and even faces—to some of the creations.

"The Simpich angels represent our children, children of friends and now grandchildren," notes Jan. "And the Cloud Babies were inspired by the birth of our third child."

The collection also includes historical and literary figures.

Some pieces are classics that return each year; others are limited editions.

"To celebrate the 50th anniversary of our marriage and business last year, we reintroduced 'O Be Joyful', a limited edition sculpture of Santa and Mrs. Claus dancing.

"The joyous message of the Christmas season is clearly etched on their faces," smiles Jan. "Of course, we hope that all of our sculptures bring joy to people year round."

Editor's Note: *For a brochure, write to Simpich Character Dolls, 2413 W. Colorado Ave., Colorado Springs CO 80904; 1-800/881-3879. Or visit the Web site at www.simpich.com.* ❉

Her Down-Home Designs Have Holiday Gifts All Sewn Up

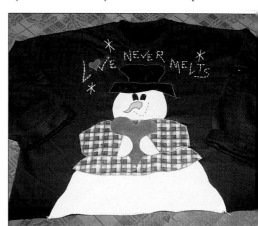

Sonya says with a chuckle.

It was her oldest daughter, Heidi, who came up with the idea of selling Sonya's shirts for extra money. Beginning with just 10 original designs, Sonya set up her sewing machine on a card table and got to work making 50 shirts for her first craft show.

Today, she sells appliqued sweatshirts, long- and short-sleeved T-shirts and denim shirts, vests, jumpers and coats at several local craft shows and also on the Internet.

Sonya's designs reflect her love of the rural farming area where she lives. "A favorite of mine is the shirt that spells out Farm Wife in letters trimmed with a tractor, red barn, cow, chicken and cornstalk," she confirms.

Her more than 50 designs include Noah's ark, scarecrows, flowers, horses, Christmas snowmen, Santas, angels, stars and much more.

"One best-selling idea was a grandma shirt that includes little wooden heart pins with the grandkids' names on them. Stanley makes all the pins for me, bless him!"

Sonya designs and cuts all appliques herself, occasionally adding a hand-stitch, buttons or doilies. Local women,

A CUT ABOVE. That's how her customers rate the cute country appliques that Sonya Johnson (left) designs and stitches to ready-made shirts, vests and coats. Daughters Holly and Elicia (below) can't get enough of Mom's artistic wearables for holiday gifts!

using industrial machines, help her applique the holiday orders. "They're all good friends and I consider them partners in the business," she adds.

But her whole extended family has pitched in over the years, says Sonya. "They help me paint, print, package orders, pick up shirts on their way home—and they put up with me in December! Our Christmases can be more than a little hectic," she confides, "but I feel so very blessed."

Editor's Note: *For a brochure, write to Sew Special Designs, 70902-438 Road, Stamford NE 68977; call 1-308/868-4471; or visit the Web site at www.megavision.com//ssd.* ❀

AS A GIRL, Sonya Johnson disliked sewing—which is hard to believe since she's stitched up her own very successful home business!

"It's funny, sometimes, the way our lives play out," muses Sonya from the 800-acre farm she shares with her husband, Stanley, in Stamford, Nebraska—only 7 miles from the dairy farm where she grew up.

"Today, sewing is an outlet for my creativity, I guess. I love to sew—except when I have a month to finish 100 orders before Christmas!"

Her home-based applique business, Sew Special Designs, began with Sonya stitching appliqued sweatshirts to give as gifts to her own four children, six grandchildren and family.

"And after 11 years they're *still* getting appliqued wearables for gifts,"

Photos: Nancy Tarkington

Santa Collectibles Catch Real Drift of Season

YOU MIGHT SAY that Marjorie Wedge Mable's childhood love of Santa Claus is all washed up...on every beach she walks, that is! For the last 18 years, this Johnston, Iowa artist has been creating fanciful Father Christmas collectibles from driftwood she finds washed up on shores and beaches.

"I'm a painter more than a carver," Marge explains, "so I use the sand-smoothed wood as my canvas. I look for

SHORING UP the spirit of Christmas with her driftwood St. Nicks is a year-round business and labor of love for artist Marjorie Mable.

wood that has some character—twists and bends and knots. The shape helps me develop each figure. Adding just the right arms and facial expression gives attitude and a unique look to each.

"Some are serious, some look tired, some have an impish twinkle in their eye, but every Santa is one-of-a-kind with its own personality. I become very partial to some as they come to life!" she adds with a laugh.

Marge made her first driftwood Santa in 1985, not long after she and daughter Jackie opened their Folk Art Shop in November of 1981 in Historic Valley Junction, a restored part of old West Des Moines and a popular tourist area.

"I'd been cutting and painting flat-wood Santas, but they needed a separate base. When I saw a piece of driftwood, I realized it could be a Santa, too. I cut it flat across the bottom and made a

free-standing figure," she recalls.

Now she enjoys spending time on the water, gathering driftwood. She carries a scrub brush and saw in her boat so she can cut and scrub each piece. After drying it in the sun, she stores it in plastic boxes until inspiration strikes.

To date, Marge has crafted more than 5,000 standing St. Nicks (about 300 a year!). They've been in the shops of New York's American Folk Art Museum, and are in personal collections across the country and even overseas.

"My Santas range from earrings less than an inch high to figures 4 feet tall, but the average is 8 to 12 inches," she notes. "Most are red, but some of my other colors include green, dark blue, white, yellow, mustard, doe beige, purple and patriotic red, white and blue."

She adds twigs from her yard for arms and paints the bodies with acrylic paint. "Next, I paint the sash, mittens, fur, face and beard. Finally, I sign, date and number each one.

"I enjoy sharing my Santas with others," confides Marge, who believes that the loving nature of Santa only enhances the real story of Christmas.

"Love is the message of Christ's coming...and there is love in the making of my Santas. I like to think my little 'ambassadors of love' help spread the message of this joyous season."

Editor's Note: *For more information, write Marge at Folk Art, 333 Fifth St., West Des Moines IA 50265; call 1-515/276-6170; or E-mail her at MWM folkart@aol.com.* ✳

Pincushion Is Sew Handy!

ON PINS and needles with all you have to decorate and craft this busy holiday season? Keep those sewing notions in one easy-to-find place—and away from curious toddlers—with this jolly Santa pincushion.

Helen Rafson of Louisville, Kentucky crafted her St. Nick from a small clay pot and fabric scraps. "He's handy for holding pushpins, too," Helen confides. "Plus, he adds a merry touch to any workroom."

Materials Needed:

Patterns at right
Tracing paper and pencil
Felt—5-1/2-inch square of white and 3-inch x 4-inch piece of apricot
3-1/2-inch-high x 3-inch-diameter clay pot
3/8-inch wooden domed furniture plug for nose
Foam plate or palette
Acrylic craft paints—pink and white
Paintbrushes—1-inch foam brush and liner
8-inch circle of red print fabric
Red all-purpose thread
Hand-sewing needle
3-inch Styrofoam ball
Two 16mm glue-on wiggle eyes
2-inch x 12-inch length of high-loft quilt batting
1-inch white pom-pom

Powdered cosmetic blush
Cotton swab
White (tacky) glue
Scissors

Finished Size: Pincushion measures about 5-1/2 inches high x 5 inches across.

Directions:

Place small amounts of paint on foam plate or palette as needed. Paint as directed, applying additional coats of paint as needed for complete coverage. Let paint dry after every application.

Using foam brush, paint entire out-side and inside rim of clay pot white and wooden furniture plug pink.

Trace patterns onto tracing paper.

Cut the beard, mustache and eyebrows from white felt and the face from apricot felt.

Glue face to one side of clay pot, positioning straight edge of face just under edge of rim.

Referring to photo for position, use cotton swab and a circular motion to apply blush to cheek area of face.

Apply a bead of glue to inner edge only of wrong side of beard. Referring to pattern for position and leaving outer edges loose, glue beard over face.

Glue mustache to face where shown on pattern, leaving ends free as shown in photo. Glue eyes, nose and eyebrows to face where shown in photo.

Use liner and white to highlight nose.

Glue batting around rim of clay pot, butting edges in back and trimming excess. Let dry.

Thread hand-sewing needle with a double strand of red thread. Sew around circle of red fabric with a running stitch about 1/4 in. from edge. See Fig. 1 for stitch illustration. Do not fasten off.

Place Styrofoam ball in center of wrong side of fabric. Pull thread to gather fabric around ball for hat. Fasten off.

Glue edges of fabric to ball as needed to hold. Let dry.

With fabric side up, glue the hat to inside of clay pot and the pom-pom to top of hat. Let dry. ★

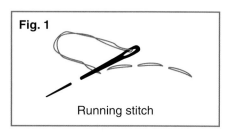

Fig. 1

Running stitch

SANTA FACE PATTERNS

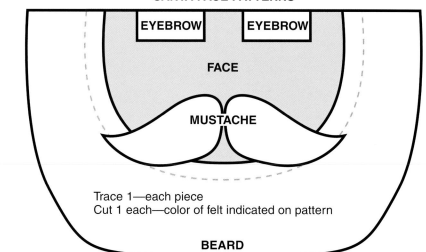

EYEBROW   EYEBROW

FACE

MUSTACHE

Trace 1—each piece
Cut 1 each—color of felt indicated on pattern

BEARD

Roly-Poly Pair Adds Flair to Homegrown Decor

HERE COME Santa and his reindeer…and oh what a gourd-geous sight! Lenora Schut of Pella, Iowa used dried gourds from her garden and a splash of paint to craft this whimsical pair.

They're sure to tickle your fancy and your funny bone, says Lenora. "I scatter them around my house or holiday buffet. And they're so inexpensive to make, you can send some home with friends."

Materials Needed (for both):
Natural dried and cleaned potbelly gourds—3-1/2-inch-high gourd for Santa and 2-inch-high gourd for reindeer
Foam plate or palette
Small container of water
Paper towel
Acrylic craft paints (Lenora used DecoArt Americana Paints)—Base Flesh, Buttermilk, Burnt Sienna, Calico Red, Camel, Dark Chocolate, Lamp Black, Sable Brown and Slate Gray
Gesso
Paintbrushes—small flat, liner, stipple brush or small stiff brush, 1-inch foam brush
Two 3/8-inch domed wooden furniture plugs for noses
Two 2-inch-long fork-shaped twigs for antlers
Black fine-line permanent marker
Powdered cosmetic blush
Cotton swab
White (tacky) glue
Drill with 1/8-inch bit
Sandpaper and tack cloth
Gloss varnish

Finished Size: Santa gourd measures about 3-1/2 inches high x 2-1/4 inches wide. Reindeer gourd measures about 3-1/2 inches high x 3-1/2 inches wide with antlers.

Directions:
Keep paper towel and a basin of water handy to clean brushes. Place dabs of each paint color onto palette or foam plate as needed. Add coats for complete coverage. Let paint dry after every application. Refer to photo at right as a guide for painting.

Sand gourds smooth and wipe clean with the tack cloth.

Use foam brush to prime gourds with gesso.

SANTA: Use flat brush and Slate Gray to paint entire 3-1/2-in. gourd.

Use flat brush and Calico Red to paint top 1-1/4 in. of gourd for hat.

Use flat brush and Base Flesh to paint a 1-1/4-in. half circle on one side of gourd for face and to completely cover one wooden furniture plug for nose.

Use liner and Buttermilk to paint mustache.

Thin Buttermilk with clean water to an ink-like consistency. Use liner to paint thinned Buttermilk swirls all around gourd for beard and hair.

Stipple a 1/2-in.-wide band of Buttermilk around bottom of hat for fur trim and a circle for pom-pom of hat, leaving gray showing around pom-pom to separate pom-pom from fur trim. To stipple, dip stipple brush or small stiff brush into Buttermilk. Tap excess paint onto palette and apply lightly with an up-and-down motion.

Glue nose in place.

Use cotton swab and a circular motion to apply cosmetic blush to cheeks and nose.

Dip smallest brush handle into Lamp Black and use to dab on two small dots for eyes and to add hat crease.

Use liner to add a tiny dot of Buttermilk to each eye for highlight.

Dip smallest brush handle into Buttermilk and use to dab on three small dots for each eyebrow.

REINDEER: Drill two holes into top of 2-in. gourd for twig antlers.

Use flat brush and Sable Brown to paint entire 2-in. gourd.

Use flat brush and Camel to paint a 1-1/4-in. x 3/4-in. rectangle with rounded corners on one side of gourd for face.

Use flat brush to add Burnt Sienna around outer edge of face to shade.

Dip smallest brush handle into Lamp Black and use to dab on two small dots above face for eyes.

Use liner to add a tiny dot of Buttermilk to each eye for highlight.

Use flat brush and Calico Red to paint wooden furniture plug for nose.

Glue nose onto face.

Use liner and Buttermilk to highlight the nose.

Use cotton swab and a circular motion to apply powdered blush to cheeks.

Using liner brush and Burnt Sienna, outline ears on sides and paint tufts of Dark Chocolate hair above eyes.

Add mouth and eyebrows with permanent marker.

Glue twigs into holes for antlers.

FINISHING: Apply varnish to both gourds following manufacturer's instructions. Let dry. Showcase your gourds!

Snowman Trim's Fit to be Tied... On Holiday Gifts or the Tree

WRAPPED UP in his warm stocking cap, this winsome fellow will melt your heart! Pam Crisler of Metairie, Louisiana used Fimo clay to craft his carrot-nosed face.

Then she added snips and tips of knit socks and gloves, and tucked him in a bag filled with cinnamon sticks, tiny pinecones, jingle bells and candy canes. The result? A winning ornament that doubles as a gift-package trim!

Materials Needed:
Patterns at right
Pencil
One royal blue cotton sock
One red knit glove
3-inch square of corrugated cardboard
36-inch length of natural raffia
Two 10-inch lengths of red all-purpose thread
Waxed paper
Rolling pin
Craft knife
Oven-bake polymer clay—brown, gold, green, orange, red and white
Straight pin or sewing needle
Two black seed beads for eyes
Powdered cosmetic blush
Cotton swab
Acrylic paints—dark blue and white
Liner paintbrush
Gold jingle bells—one 1/2-inch and one 1/8-inch

Five 3-inch-long sprigs of artificial evergreen
Two 3-inch-long cinnamon sticks
Two 5/8-inch-long pinecones
Buttons—one 5/8-inch gray and one 1/2-inch red ball button
Glue gun and glue sticks
Ruler
Scissors

Finished Size: Snowman trim measures about 5 inches wide x 7 inches tall.

Directions:
Cut across sock 5 in. from end of cuff. Discard foot portion of sock.

Gather cut edge of cuff in your hand. Working with the two red threads as one, tightly wrap thread around cuff about 1 in. from cut edge. Tie thread ends in a bow. Trim ends as desired.

Turn upper (finished) cuff edge down about 1 in.

Trim cardboard piece to width of cuff if needed. Round corners of one end of cardboard with scissors. Insert rounded end of cardboard into cuff.

Apply a bead of glue to cardboard inside cuff about 1 in. from top edge to hold cardboard in place. Do not apply glue above the 1-in. mark. This area is needed to insert the decorations.

Cut a 6-in. length of raffia for hanger. Glue ends of raffia to back of cardboard at each upper corner.

Knead the clay until soft and smooth, making sure to wash your hands each time you use a new color of clay. To prevent the colors of clay from mixing, work each color on a separate sheet of waxed paper.

Roll a 1-in. ball of white clay and form into a slightly flattened oval for head.

Referring to photo for placement, press two black seed beads into head for eyes.

Form a 3/8-in.-long carrot shape nose from orange clay and press into place on head.

Use pin or needle to indent dots for mouth and to make eyebrows on head where shown in photo.

Use cotton swab and a circular motion to apply blush to cheeks.

Trace star and gingerbread man patterns onto waxed paper.

Place a small piece of gold clay between two pieces of waxed paper. Roll

out clay with rolling pin until about 1/8 in. thick. Place star pattern on clay and cut out star with craft knife. Roll out brown clay and cut gingerbread man in same way.

To form candy cane, roll a 2-in.-long x 1/8-in.-thick rope each of white, green and red clay. Carefully twist the three ropes together and roll until smooth. Cut a 2-in.-long piece and shape it into a candy cane as shown in photo.

To make peppermint stick, roll and twist a piece of white and red clay as for candy cane. Cut a 2-in.-long piece and leave straight for peppermint stick.

To make peppermint candies, roll four 1-in.-long x 1/8-in.-thick ropes of red clay and five of white clay. Press red and white clay ropes onto side of a white clay rope, alternating colors to make one 1-in.-long rope. Roll the joined rope together until smooth and about 3/8 in. in diameter. Cut three 1/8-in.-thick slices from the rope.

Bake all clay pieces following manufacturer's directions. Let cool.

Use liner to add white wavy lines to gingerbread man's arms and legs. Add a smile, eyes and hair using white paint. Let dry.

Use liner and dark blue to add dots for eyes. Let dry.

Cut a 2-in. length from one finger of red glove for hat. Fold cut edge up about 5/8 in. and glue hat onto top of head.

Referring to photo for placement, glue star and smaller gold jingle bell onto front of hat.

Referring to photo for placement, glue cinnamon sticks, pine boughs, candy cane and peppermint stick to front of cardboard piece inside cuff. Glue head to the right side of cuff and pinecones to the right of the head. Glue gingerbread man on left side and peppermint candies and bell where shown.

Tie remaining raffia into a bow. Glue bow to left side of cuff. Glue gray button to center of raffia bow and red ball button to center of gray button.

Use to trim a package or hang from your Christmas tree! ★

SNOWMAN TRIM PATTERNS

GINGERBREAD MAN
Trace 1—waxed paper
Cut 1—brown clay

STAR
Trace 1—waxed paper
Cut 1—gold clay

Trim Candles in Holiday Style

THESE holly-jolly foam candle huggers are sure to dress up any holiday table or snowy window! Crafter Verlyn King of Tremonton, Utah includes patterns for a jaunty holly sprig and be-whiskered St. Nick.

"These trims are easy to make, and you can design your own simple shapes, like stars or Christmas trees," she says.

Materials Needed (for holly and Santa trims):

Patterns below
Tracing paper and pencil
Ballpoint pen
Craft foam—scraps each of flesh, red and white for Santa candle hugger and green and red for holly candle hugger
Scrap of lightweight cardboard
1/4-inch round paper punch
Two 5mm glue-on wiggle eyes
Acrylic craft paints—red and white
Small round paintbrush
Cotton swab
Paper towel
Glue stick
Low-temperature glue gun and glue sticks
Black fine-line permanent marker (Verlyn used a Sharpie marker)
Scissors
Two 12-inch red taper candles

Finished Size: Santa candle hugger measures about 2 inches across x 3-1/2 inches high. Holly leaf candle hugger

measures about 3 inches across x 2-1/4 inches high.

Directions:

Trace patterns including dashed lines onto tracing paper with pencil. Use glue stick to glue patterns onto lightweight cardboard. Cut out patterns on traced lines.

Trace around patterns onto craft foam with ballpoint pen as directed on patterns. Cut out shapes, cutting just inside traced lines.

SANTA: Referring to pattern for position, glue hat and beard centered along back of hat brim with straight edges of hat and beard pieces meeting. Glue white circle to tip of hat. Let dry.

Use paper punch to cut nose from flesh craft foam. Glue nose to bottom of face.

Dip cotton swab into red paint and blot on paper towel to remove excess paint. With a circular motion, apply paint to cheeks and top half of nose.

Glue face to right side of beard under hat brim.

Glue wiggle eyes to face just above nose.

Referring to photo for placement, use round brush and white paint to add eyebrows. Let dry.

Using black marker, lightly outline beard, face, nose and hat with straight lines. Outline hat brim and white circle with squiggly lines.

Form white craft foam hugger strip into a ring. Adjust ring to fit around candle where desired by overlapping short

ends. Glue ends to hold. Glue ring across back of Santa where hat and beard meet behind hat brim.

HOLLY LEAVES: Referring to photo for placement, use black marker to draw veins on one side of holly leaves and to outline edges. Add dashed line around each berry.

Use liner and white to highlight each holly berry.

Form a ring from green craft foam hugger strip as for Santa.

Referring to photo for position, glue holly leaves right side up to green ring with narrow ends of leaves pointing up and outward. Glue holly berries to bottom of leaves as shown in photo.

Dress up your Christmas candles!

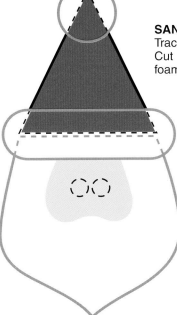

SANTA PATTERN
Trace 1 each piece—tracing paper
Cut 1 each piece—color of craft foam shown on patterns

HOLLY BERRY PATTERN
Trace 1—tracing paper
Cut 2—red craft foam

HUGGER STRIP PATTERN
Trace 1—tracing paper
Cut 1 each—green and white craft foam

HOLLY LEAF PATTERN
Trace 1—tracing paper
Cut 2—green craft foam

Gingerbread Garland Strings Out A Warm Down-Home Welcome

TRIM THE TREE or deck a doorway with this homespun garland of gingerbread kids. "The possibilities are endless," comments crafter Julie Todd of Aurelia, Iowa.

Easy directions show how to spice up Julie's cute felt figures with beads, buttons, bows and a pinch of imagination! The garland looks especially pretty when twined with grapevine or evergreen boughs.

Materials Needed:
Patterns on next page
Tracing paper and pencil
Quilter's marking pen or pencil
Eighteen 6-1/2-inch x 7-inch pieces of light brown felt
1/8 yard of 44-inch-wide Christmas plaid fabric
All-purpose thread to match felt and plaid fabric
Dimensional fabric/craft paints—black, red and white
Forty 1/2-inch red wooden beads
Ten 3/4-inch-tall x 5/8-inch-diameter natural wooden spools
Green acrylic craft paint and small flat paintbrush
Two-hole buttons—ten 1/2-inch green buttons and eight 1/2-inch red buttons
White heavy thread or crochet cotton
5-1/2-inch x 7-inch piece of paper-backed fusible web
3 yards of 1/4-inch-wide red satin ribbon
White (tacky) glue
Standard sewing supplies

Finished Size: Garland is about 9 feet long. Each gingerbread shape is about 6-1/2 inches tall x 5-3/4 inches wide.

Directions:
GINGERBREAD SHAPES: Trace gingerbread pattern onto tracing paper with pencil. Cut out pattern on traced lines.

Using quilter's marking pen or pencil, trace around gingerbread pattern onto one side of nine pieces of brown felt.

Place each traced gingerbread shape right side up on another piece of brown felt. Pin layers together with edges matching.

Using matching thread, machine-sew on traced line around each gingerbread shape.

Cut out each, cutting 1/4 in. outside stitching line through both layers of felt.

Turn gingerbread shapes over when adding remaining details so tracing lines do not show on the front.

Cut a 1-in. x 36-in. strip of plaid fabric. Cut strip into nine 4-in.-long pieces. Tie an overhand knot in the center of each piece. Trim ends to make a 2-1/2-in.-long bow with knot in middle. Pull threads to fray ends. Repeat to make eight more bows. Set bows aside.

Cut four 2-1/2-in. x 4-in. rectangles from the plaid fabric for aprons. Thread needle with matching thread and sew a gathering stitch near one long edge of each fabric rectangle. Pull thread and knot each end so the gathered edge of each is about 1-1/2 in. long. Set aprons aside.

Trace five hearts onto the paper side of fusible web with pencil, leaving 1/2 in. between shapes. Cut shapes apart, leaving a margin of paper around each.

With grain lines matching, fuse shapes onto wrong side of a scrap of plaid fabric. Cut out hearts on traced lines.

Remove paper backing. Referring to photo above for placement, fuse a heart onto five gingerbread shapes.

PAINTING: Referring to the pattern and photo for placement, add a double wavy line of white dimensional paint across legs, arms and heads of the five gingerbread (boy) shapes with hearts. Let dry.

Paint a single wavy outline of white dimensional paint over stitching line on the remaining four gingerbread (girl) shapes. Let dry.

Use black dimensional paint to add eyes and a smile to each gingerbread shape. Let dry.

Use red dimensional paint to add dots for cheeks to all faces. Let dry.

Paint wooden spools green. Let dry.

FINISHING: Cut ten 1/2-in. x 2-in. pieces of plaid fabric. Glue a fabric piece around each painted spool. Let dry.

Referring to photo for placement, glue a bow to the neck of each gingerbread boy. Glue a bow to the head of each gingerbread girl.

Glue the gathered edge of an apron

to the waist of each gingerbread girl.

Thread a needle with white heavy thread or crochet cotton. Insert needle from front to back and then from back to front of a button. Tie ends in a knot on the front of the button. Trim ends to 1/4 in. Repeat for all of the remaining buttons.

Referring to pattern for placement, glue two green buttons to each gingerbread boy and two red buttons to each gingerbread girl. Let dry.

ASSEMBLY: Thread two red beads, one spool and two more red beads onto the red ribbon. Secure the first bead about 12 in. from the end of the ribbon by inserting the ribbon through the bead again and tying the ribbon around the bead.

With the beads pushed tightly together, glue the ribbon across back of the arms of a gingerbread boy, leaving 1/8 in. between the end of the arm and the beads for flexibility of garland.

Thread two red beads, one spool and two more red beads on the ribbon. Glue the ribbon across the back of the arms of a gingerbread girl as before. Add beads and spool as before. Repeat, alternating remaining gingerbread boys and girls and beads and spools.

Secure last bead by inserting the ribbon through the bead again and tying the ribbon around the bead.

Trim ribbon ends, leaving about 10 in. of ribbon at each end.

Hang your gingerbread garland on a fireplace mantel or on a Christmas tree!

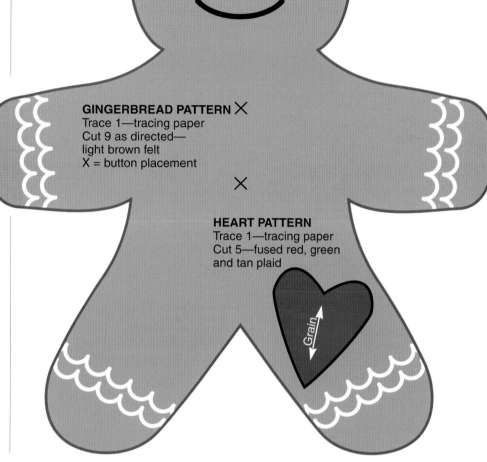

GINGERBREAD PATTERN X
Trace 1—tracing paper
Cut 9 as directed—
light brown felt
X = button placement

HEART PATTERN
Trace 1—tracing paper
Cut 5—fused red, green and tan plaid

Grain

Tradition Focuses Family on Love

"OUR FAMILY shares many special holiday traditions, but there's one that inspires all of us, adults and children alike, to get into the true Christmas spirit," writes Adelaide Krumm of Manasquan, New Jersey.

"On the first Sunday of Advent, I set up our Nativity with the figures of Mary and Joseph…but no Baby Jesus. Next to the empty crib, I place a bag made of holiday fabric that's filled with straw. The bag can be any size you want—mine is about 12 by 14 inches.

"Near the scene, I place a small basket containing red slips of paper with suggestions for kind acts the children can do. These range from household chores to helping a neighbor to calling a truce with a sibling for the day. The ideas are as endless as our imaginations, and we encourage the children to contribute many of their own suggestions.

"As for the adults in the family, their ideas for random acts of kindness are written on green slips of paper and include things like volunteering to ring a bell for the Salvation Army, collecting items for the local food bank or visiting a shut-in.

"Each day during Advent, family members choose a slip of paper from the basket and do a good deed for others," explains Adelaide. "Then the 'good Samaritans' can take a straw or two from the bag and place it in the manger.

"By Christmas Eve, Baby Jesus' crib is filled with straw, and we gather as a family to place him in his soft bed. Sometimes, we celebrate the event with a carol or a Bible reading. Always, it's a wonderful reminder to us all of the season's greatest gift—love."

Spruce Up the Season by Stitching an Evergreen Quilt

NO MATTER how frightful the weather, this queen-sized quilt will bundle up the holidays in toasty memories. Using scraps of Christmases past provided by her daughter, quilter Gwen Hahn of Eunice, New Mexico created a forest of festive firs and a lasting family keepsake with this quilt.

"I got my idea for the tree designs from a coloring book," Gwen confides. She added round or angular stars and trunks to each tree, and shiny garlands of gold or silver.

Materials Needed:

Patterns on next page
Tracing paper and pencil
Scissors
44-inch-wide 100% cotton fabrics—
  5 yards of white solid for quilt
  blocks, 8-3/4 yards of green solid
  for sashing and border strips and
  for backing, 1/2 yard of red solid for
  corner squares and 1/8 yard each
  or scraps of yellow solid and brown
  solid for stars and tree trunks
Forty-two 10-inch squares of several
  different 100% cotton Christmas
  print fabrics for tree appliques
  (Gwen used six different prints)
85-inch x 98-inch piece of lightweight
  quilt batting
Forty-two 9-1/2-inch squares plus 1/2
  yard of paper-backed fusible web
All-purpose thread—green, red and
  white
White hand-quilting thread
Six-strand embroidery floss—brown,
  green, red and yellow
Embroidery needle
Quilter's marking pen or pencil
Quilter's ruler
  Rotary cutter and mat (optional)
  Standard sewing supplies

Finished Size: The quilt measures about 81 inches wide x 94 inches long.

Directions:

Pre-wash fabrics, washing each color separately. If rinse water is discolored, wash again until rinse water runs clear. Dry and press fabrics.

Do all piecing with accurate 1/4-in. seams, edges matching and right sides of fabrics together unless otherwise directed. Press seams toward darker fabric when possible.

CUTTING: Accurately cut fabrics using a rotary cutter and quilter's ruler or mark fabrics using a ruler and marker of choice and cut with scissors.

From white solid, cut forty-two 12-in. squares for appliqued blocks.

From green solid, cut and set aside a 6-yard length for backing. From remaining fabric, cut ninety-seven 3-in. x 11-in. pieces for sashing and border strips.

From red solid, cut fifty-six 3-in. squares for corners.

APPLIQUES: Mark tracing paper with a 1-in. grid and draw patterns onto tracing paper as shown. Or use copy machine to enlarge patterns to 200%.

Trace around patterns onto folded tracing paper. Cut out each on traced lines and unfold for complete patterns.

Trace around rounded and pointed tree trunks and stars 21 times each onto paper side of fusible web, leaving a 1/2-in. margin between shapes. Cut shapes apart.

Following manufacturer's directions, fuse star shapes onto yellow solid fabric and tree trunk shapes onto brown solid fabric with grain lines matching. Cut out shapes on traced lines.

Fuse a 9-1/2-in. square of paper-backed fusible web centered onto wrong side of each 10-in. square of Christmas print fabric.

With grain lines matching, trace around rounded and pointed tree patterns onto fused Christmas print fabrics as directed on patterns. Cut out each on traced lines. Remove paper backing.

Referring to photo for placement, place a rounded tree trunk, tree and star right side up on the right side of a 12-in. white solid fabric square, overlapping pieces as shown in photo. Fuse pieces in place.

Repeat to make a total of 21 rounded trees and 21 pointed trees.

EMBROIDERY: Separate six-strand floss and use two strands to blanket-stitch around each tree trunk with brown floss. See Fig. 1 for stitch illustration. Then blanket-stitch around each tree with either red or green floss and around each star with yellow floss.

Use two strands of green or red floss to chain-stitch rows of garland on each tree where shown on the patterns. See

Fig. 1 for stitch illustration.

Trim each appliqued and embroidered block to an accurate 11-in. square with trees centered.

PIECING: Lay out appliqued blocks right side up, alternating rounded and pointed appliqued trees in seven rows with six blocks in each row with green sashing strips and red corner squares. See Fig. 2.

Keeping the rest of layout intact, sew first row of sashing strips and corner squares together. Then sew blocks and sashing strips in next row together in planned order.

In same way, sew each remaining row together.

Sew a pieced sashing strip to the top of the first pieced row, carefully matching corners.

Then add remaining pieced sashing strips and pieced rows as planned to complete the pieced top.

MARKING: Use quilter's marking pen or pencil to mark five horizontal lines 1-3/4 in. apart and a vertical line 1 in. from the side seams on each appliqued block.

Then mark sashing strips and corner blocks with quilting design of choice.

QUILTING: Cut 6-yd. length of backing fabric in half crosswise. Trim selvage edges and sew the long edges together with a 1/2-in. seam. Press seam open. Trim to make an 85-in. x 98-in. piece with seam centered.

Place backing wrong side up on a flat surface. Center the batting over the backing and smooth out. With right side up, center pieced top over batting and smooth out.

Hand-baste from center to corners, then horizontally and vertically every 4 in. and 1/4 in. from outside edge.

With white quilting thread, hand-quilt over marked quilting lines and around each tree.

BINDING: Trim batting only 1/4 in. from edge of quilt top. Trim backing, leaving a 3/4-in. margin of backing fabric around all sides.

Press 1/4 in. to wrong side around all edges of backing.

Fold backing to front along top edge, encasing raw edges and overlapping raw edge of quilt top 1/4 in. With matching thread, hand-sew fold of backing to front of quilt top.

Repeat along bottom edge and then along opposite side edges.

Remove basting and marked quilting lines.

Give as a gift to a special friend...or use this warm and woodsy covering to brighten a room in your own home for the holidays!

Enlarge pattern 200%
Each square = 1 in.

TREE QUILT PATTERNS

ROUNDED TREE STAR
Trace 1 as directed—
folded tracing paper
Cut 21—fused yellow solid

POINTED TREE STAR
Trace 1 as directed—
folded tracing paper
Cut 21—fused yellow solid

Foldline

Foldline

Foldline
Grain

Foldline
Grain

ROUNDED TREE
Trace 1 as directed—
folded tracing paper
Cut 21—different fused
Christmas prints

POINTED TREE
Trace 1 as directed—
folded tracing paper
Cut 21—different fused
Christmas prints

Foldline
Grain

Foldline
Grain

POINTED TREE TRUNK
Trace 1 as directed—
folded tracing paper
Cut 21—fused brown solid

ROUNDED TREE TRUNK
Trace 1 as directed—folded tracing paper
Cut 21—fused brown solid

APPLIQUE KEY
— Outline
- - - Overlapped part of pattern
— Inside design line

Fig. 1

Blanket stitch

Chain stitch

Fig. 2 Layout

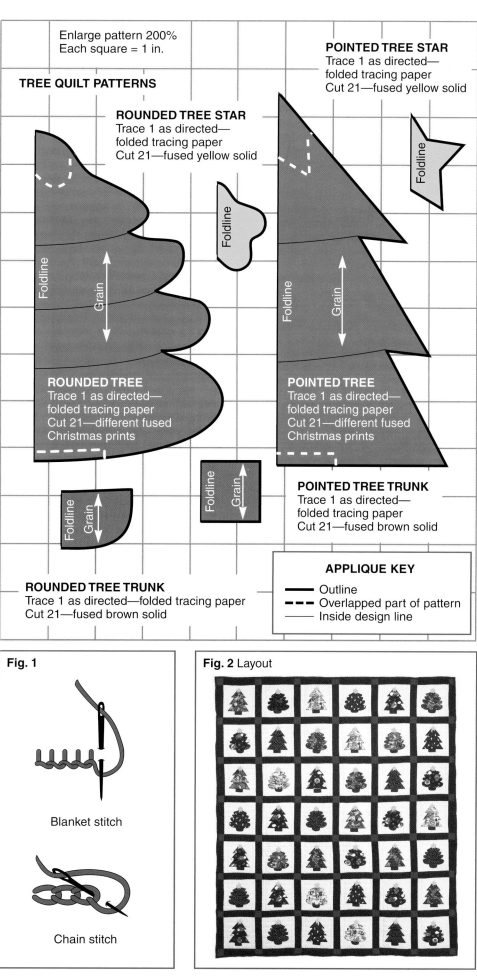

Snowflake Has Season Pinned

IF YOU'RE dreaming of a white Christmas, you'll love this novel snowflake pin. Created by crafter Bette Veinot of Bridgewater, Nova Scotia, it glistens just like the real thing.

"These pins are so quick and easy to make," Betty says. "You'll want to whip up a storm of them—especially for those folks and friends who don't like going out in the cold!"

Materials Needed:
1-3/4-inch-high x 3/16-inch-thick
  purchased wooden snowflake
Foam plate or palette
Paper towels
Acrylic craft paints—black, rose and
  white
Textured snow medium
Clear iridescent varnish (Bette used
  Delta Sparkle Glaze)
Paintbrushes—1-inch foam brush,
  small flat and liner
Toothpick
1-inch pin back
Glue gun and glue stick

Finished Size: Pin measures about 1-3/4 inches high x 1-3/4 inches wide.

Directions:
Place small amounts of paint on foam plate or palette as needed. Apply additional coats of paint as needed for complete coverage. Let paint dry after every application.

Refer to the photo above right as a guide while painting as directed in the instructions that follow.

Use foam brush and white to paint snowflake.

Use liner and black to paint eyes, lashes and eyebrows.

Use liner and white to add a highlight to each eye.

Dip toothpick into white and dab one dot in center of each eye and one dot at bottom of white highlight on eye.

Dip toothpick into rose and use to dab two dots on face for nose. While paint is still wet, use toothpick to pull down paint dots to make a small heart.

Dip flat brush into rose paint and wipe on paper towel until nearly dry. Dab a circle on each side of nose for cheeks.

Use liner and black to add mouth, extending mouth lines onto cheeks.

Use foam brush to apply iridescent varnish following manufacturer's instructions.

Apply textured snow with toothpick, referring to photo for placement. Let dry.

Glue pin back centered on back of snowflake.

Pin on someone you love! ★

Tiny Patchwork Pillows Double as Sachets

VISIONS of sugarplums couldn't be sweeter than these tiny patchwork puffs tied up with jingle bells and shiny ribbon! Mary Lou Nash from Elmer, Louisiana uses them as tree trimmers

and suggests, "Make them in a variety of shapes by using different cookie-cutter patterns."

She stuffs her pillows with batting, but you can also fill them with potpourri or lavender to turn them into sweet-smelling sachets.

Materials Needed (for one):
100% cotton or cotton-blend fabrics—
  two 2-1/2-inch squares each of two
  different coordinating Christmas
  prints for pieced front and one
  4-1/2-inch square of coordinating
  or matching fabric for back
1/8-inch-wide or 1/4-inch-wide satin
  ribbon—4-inch length of green or
  white for hanger and 8-inch length
  of red or white for bow
Matching all-purpose thread
Polyester fiberfill
1/2-inch gold jingle bell
Standard sewing supplies

Finished Size: Each ornament measures about 4 inches square without hanger.

Directions:
Lay out the 2-1/2-in. squares right side

up in two rows with two squares in each row as shown in the photo at left.

With right sides together, sew the squares in each row together with a 1/4-in. seam. Press seams toward darker fabrics.

To form a four-patch square, sew the two rows together as planned with a 1/4-in. seam, carefully matching corners. Press seam open.

Cut 4-in. length of ribbon for hanger. Fold ribbon in half. With raw edges even, pin ribbon to right side of one corner of four-patch square.

Pin the four-patch square and 4-1/2-in. square of backing fabric together with raw edges even and ribbon hanger between layers. Sew layers together with a 1/4-in. seam, leaving an opening for turning along one edge. Trim corners diagonally.

Turn right side out and press. Stuff ornament lightly with fiberfill. Turn raw edges of opening in and hand-sew opening closed.

Tie remaining length of ribbon in a small bow. With matching thread, hand-sew ribbon to center of four-patch square and jingle bell to center of bow.

Hang on your Christmas tree! ★

Crocheted Table Topper Adds Very Merry Christmas Note

A CHEERY old-time table topper designed by Connie Folse of Thibodaux, Louisiana brings a nostalgic touch of Christmas color to any holiday setting.

"It's a cinch to crochet—even for beginners," Connie promises. With a little help from an adult, even youngsters can create a "made from the heart" gift that their parents or grandparents will cherish and keep.

Materials Needed:
4-ply worsted-weight yarn—2 ounces
  each of green, red and white
Size H/8 (5mm) crochet hook or size
  needed to obtain correct gauge
Tapestry or yarn needle
Scissors

Gauge: 4 scs and 3 rows = 1 inch.

Finished Size: Table scarf measures about 18 inches across.

Directions:
Round 1: With white yarn, ch 2, (lp on hk does not count as a ch), work 6 scs in second ch from hk, join with a sl st in first sc: 6 scs.

Round 2: Ch 1, work 2 scs in each sc around, join with a sl st in first sc. Fasten off: 12 scs.

Round 3: With green yarn and a sl knot on hk, sc in joining st of Round 2, [ch 3, sk next st, sc in next st] 5 times, ch 3, sk next st, join with a sl st in first sc: 6 ch-3 sps.

Round 4: Ch 1, work 1 sc in first st, [work 6 scs in next ch-3 sp, work 1 sc in next sc] 5 times, work 6 scs in last ch-3 sp, join with a sl st in first sc. Fasten off: 42 scs.

Round 5: With white yarn and a sl knot on hk, work 1 sc in fourth sc of first 6-sc group, [ch 6, work 1 sc in fourth sc of next 6-sc group] 5 times, ch 6, join with a sl st in first sc: 6 ch-6 sps.

Round 6: Ch 1, [work 1 sc in sc, work 8 scs in next ch-6 sp] 6 times, join with a sl st in first sc. Fasten off: 54 scs.

Round 7: With green yarn and a sl knot on hk, sc in first sc of Round 6, [work 1 hdc in each of next 8 scs, work 1 sc in next sc] 5 times, work 1 hdc in each of next 8 scs, join with a sl st in first sc: 54 sts.

Round 8: Ch 1, * work 1 sc in each of next 5 sts, work 2 scs in next st; repeat from * around, join with a sl st in first sc. Fasten off: 63 scs.

Round 9: With white yarn and a sl knot on hk, sc in first sc of Round 8, work 1 sc in each of next 5 scs, work 2 scs in next sc, * work 1 sc in each of next 6 scs, work 2 scs in next sc; repeat from * around, join with a sl st in first st: 72 scs.

Round 10: Ch 1, * work 2 scs in next st, work 1 sc in each of next 7 sts; repeat from * around, join with a sl st in first sc. Fasten off: 81 scs.

Round 11: With red yarn and a sl knot on hk, sc in first st of Round 10, work 1 sc in each st around, join with a sl st in first sc: 81 scs.

Round 12: Ch 1, * work 1 sc in each of next 3 sts, ch 7, sk next 6 sts; repeat from * around, join with a sl st in first st: 9 ch-7 sps.

Round 13: Ch 1, * work 1 sc in each of next 3 scs, work 9 scs in next ch-7 sp; repeat from * around, join with a sl st in first sc. Fasten off: 108 scs.

Round 14: With white yarn and a sl knot on hk, sc in first sc of Round 13, work 1 sc in each st around, join with a sl st in first sc: 108 scs.

Round 15: Ch 1, * work 1 sc in each of the next 11 sts, work 2 scs in next st; repeat from * around, join with a sl st in first sc. Fasten off: 117 scs.

Round 16: With green yarn and a sl knot on hk, sc in first sc of Round 15, * work 1 sc in each of the next 12 sts, work 2 scs in next st; repeat from * around, join with a sl st in first sc: 126 scs.

Round 17: Ch 1, * work 1 sc in each of next 3 scs, ch 7, sk next 6 sts; repeat from * around, join with a sl st in first sc: 14 ch-7 sps.

Round 18: Repeat Round 13. Fasten off: 168 scs.

Round 19: Join white yarn with a sl st in first st of Round 18, ch 1, * work 1 sc in each of next 3 scs, work 1 hdc in each of next 9 scs; repeat from * around, join with a sl st in first sc: 168 sts.

Round 20: Ch 1, * work 1 sc in each of next 13 sts, work 2 scs in next st; repeat from * around, join with a sl st in first st. Fasten off: 180 sts.

Round 21: With red yarn and a sl knot on hk, sc in first st of Round 20, work 1 sc in each st around, join with a sl st in first sc: 180 sts.

Round 22: Repeat Round 17: 20 ch-7 sps.

Round 23: Repeat Round 13: Fasten off: 240 sts.

Round 24: With white yarn, sl st in first st of Round 23, ch 1, * work 1 sc in each of next 3 scs, work 1 hdc in each of next 9 scs; repeat from * around, join with a sl st in first st. Fasten off: 240 sts.

Use a tapestry needle to weave in loose yarn ends. ★

ABBREVIATIONS

ch(s)	chain(s)
hk	hook
hdc(s)	half double crochet(s)
lp	loop
sc(s)	single crochet(s)
sk	skip
sl	slip
sl st	slip stitch
sp(s)	space(s)
st(s)	stitch(es)
* or [ ]	Instructions following asterisk or within brackets are repeated as directed.

Kids Will Warm Up to St. Nick Sweatshirt

DECK your little darlings in North-Pole style with this easy Santa sweatshirt. The applique, designed by Donna Stefanik of Westfield, Massachusetts, sports a real bell that kids love to jingle!

"I like using the buttonhole stitch because of the country look it lends," advises Donna, "but crafters could machine-applique or outline the shapes with dimensional paints, too."

Materials Needed:
Patterns on next page
Tracing paper and pencil
Scissors
Dark green cotton/polyester blend sweatshirt
100% cotton or cotton-blend fabrics—1/8 yard each or scraps of white-on-white print, yellow print, red pin-dot, tan solid, dark red solid and black solid
1/2 yard of paper-backed fusible web
1/2-inch gold jingle bell
Black six-strand embroidery floss
Embroidery needle
Standard sewing supplies

Finished Size: Design is 8-1/2 inches high x 9-1/2 inches wide and is shown on a Child size Medium sweatshirt.

Directions:
Pre-wash all fabrics without fabric softeners, washing colors separately. If the water from any fabric is discolored, wash again until rinse water runs clear. Dry and press all fabrics.

Wash and dry sweatshirt following manufacturer's instructions.

Trace Santa and star patterns onto paper side of fusible web as directed on patterns, leaving 1/2 in. between shapes. Cut shapes apart, leaving a margin of paper around each.

Fuse shapes onto wrong side of fabrics as directed on patterns with grain lines matching and following manufacturer's directions. Cut out the shapes on traced lines.

Remove paper backing from shapes and place them right side up on the front of the sweatshirt as shown in the photo at right and overlapping shapes as shown on pattern. Fuse shapes in place.

Separate six-strand floss and thread needle with three strands. Backstitch around whites of eyes and blanket-stitch around remaining shapes. See Fig. 1 on next page for stitch illustrations.

Hand-sew jingle bell to tip of Santa's hat.

"Model" on a child or grandchild for a festive gathering. ★

Pixies Pack Plenty of Holiday Cheer

Editor's Note: *This charming tradition for celebrating the 12 Days of Christmas was sent in by a family who wants to remain anonymous. We're more than happy to comply since we don't want to spoil the fun for them…or for their lucky recipients!*

EVERY NOVEMBER, each of our children selects a family in town to "pixie". Starting about December 12th, we begin our secret mission—delivering a holiday treat to those on the list.

The first night, we might leave a popcorn wreath or an apple pie. The second evening, we give two of something, such as two chocolate bells, and so on.

We continue our secret stops until the 12th night, when we usually slip a dozen cinnamon buns in the shape of a Christmas tree on the front porch.

It's hard to figure out ways to leave the goodies without getting caught, but that's also part of the fun. The kids love it and even the littlest ones can run pretty fast after they drop off a treat!

When we first began this tradition of pixie-ing, we would ring the doorbell on the last night and reveal who we were. But since moving to a smaller town, we no longer do that.

We've discovered that even in the pixie game, practice makes perfect…or almost perfect, anyway. We've been caught on only two occasions—out of about 30 over the years.

One Christmas, our youngsters chose to pixie the family of one of my co-workers. It was hard not to let on, especially with the whole staff abuzz trying to figure out who the secret Santa was. But I just sat silently and listened.

My colleague tried everything to catch us in the act, including staying up past 11 p.m. on the second to the last night, but our pixie-ing prowess prevailed!

Playing "pixie" to our friends and neighbors has become a treasured part of the holidays for our family and has given us many fun memories we love to re-live each year.

TRADITIONAL, TOO? *Have a fun holiday Christmas tradition you'd like to share in a future book? Send the details, plus color photos if possible, to Traditions, Country Woman Christmas, 5925 Country Lane, Greendale WI 53129. Include a self-addressed stamped envelope if you'd like your photos returned.* ★

KID'S APPLIQUE SHIRT PATTERNS

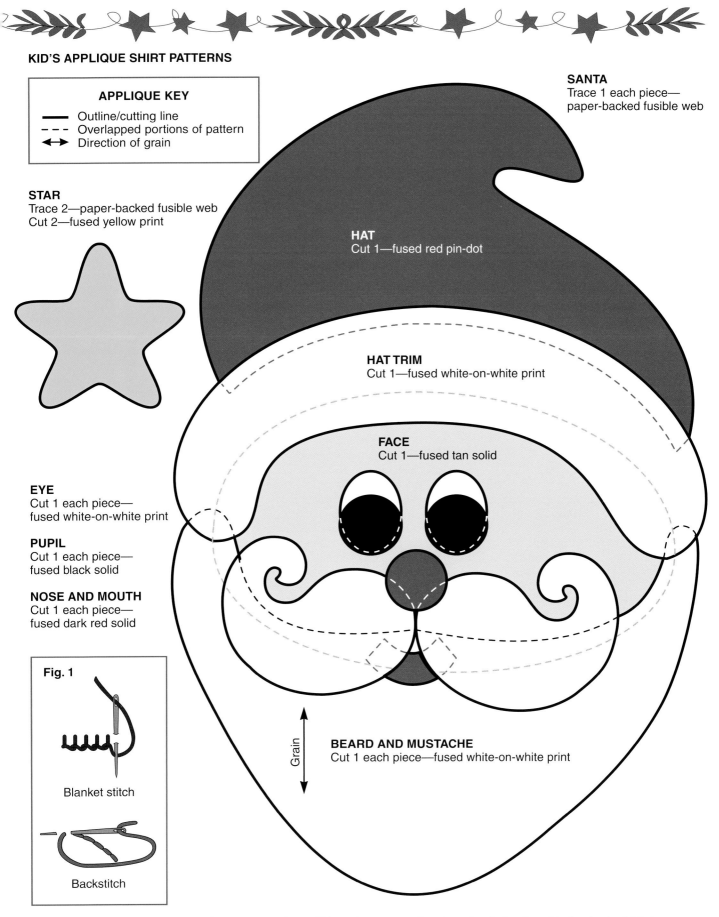

APPLIQUE KEY

— Outline/cutting line
- - - Overlapped portions of pattern
↔ Direction of grain

STAR
Trace 2—paper-backed fusible web
Cut 2—fused yellow print

SANTA
Trace 1 each piece—
paper-backed fusible web

HAT
Cut 1—fused red pin-dot

HAT TRIM
Cut 1—fused white-on-white print

FACE
Cut 1—fused tan solid

EYE
Cut 1 each piece—
fused white-on-white print

PUPIL
Cut 1 each piece—
fused black solid

NOSE AND MOUTH
Cut 1 each piece—
fused dark red solid

Fig. 1

Blanket stitch

Backstitch

Grain

BEARD AND MUSTACHE
Cut 1 each piece—fused white-on-white print

Note: Patterns are shown in reverse so they will face the correct direction after being fused to the back of fabrics.

Trims Fit Pint-Size Givers

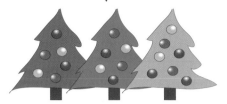

KIDS LOVE the quick turn-around time on these cute trims, confides Mary Cosgrove of Rockville, Connecticut. But family and friends will cherish the photos inside for years to come.

Mary's easy-to-follow directions will help children turn chenille stems into merry snowmen or angel ornaments or magnets that they'll take pride in making and giving.

Materials Needed (for both):

6mm pipe cleaners (chenille stems)— one 12-inch length of white and two 6-inch lengths each of red or green for snowman; one 12-inch length each of light blue and yellow, one 6-inch length of pink and 4-inch length of yellow for angel

Two 6-inch lengths of nylon thread or two 1-inch lengths of 1/2-inch-wide magnetic strip

8-inch length of 1/4-inch-wide white satin ribbon for angel

White (tacky) glue

Ruler

Scissors

Small photos

Finished Size: Each snowman measures about 2-1/2 inches across x 4-3/8 inches high, excluding hanger. Angel measures about 3-3/4 inches across x 5 inches high.

Directions:

SNOWMAN: Overlap the ends of white pipe cleaner about 1/2 in. and twist the ends around each other to hold, forming a large circle.

With twisted ends on top, twist large circle to form a figure eight with a 1-1/4-in. circle on top for head and a larger cir-

cle on the bottom as shown in photo. Twist the pipe cleaner between the two circles again to hold.

For hat, overlap the ends of one 6-in.-long green or red pipe cleaner about 1 in. Place the hat on top of the head circle and twist each end under the head and through the hat, leaving ends of hat for brim on each side. Shape loop to form a hat and straighten ends for brim as shown in photo.

For scarf, fold remaining 6-in.-long green or red pipe cleaner in half. Place fold on right side between head and body of snowman with one end of scarf in front and the other end in back. Bring back end through the large circle and twist both ends under the snowman's head at front.

At left side of snowman, twist ends around the top of the other side of the circle, leaving about 1 in. for ends of the scarf. Shape ends as desired.

Cut photo the size of snowman's head with subject of photo centered. Apply a bead of glue to the back of pipe cleaner head. Center right side of photo on back of head. Let dry.

Glue magnetic strip centered on back of photo, or tie nylon thread to top of hat for hanger.

ANGEL: Mark center of 12-in.-long yellow pipe cleaner. Fold pipe cleaner on each side 2-1/4 in. from center, bringing pipe cleaner ends toward center and twisting the ends around center to secure. Shape pipe cleaner to form wings as shown in photo.

For head, form 6-in.-long pink pipe cleaner into a 1-1/4-in. circle. With the wing ends pointing upward, twist the ends of the pink pipe cleaner around the center of the wings to attach head to wings.

Twist ends of 4-in.-long yellow pipe cleaner around top of head and shape into an oval for halo as shown in photo.

To make the angel's gown, twist the ends of the 12-in.-long light blue pipe cleaner around the center of the wings below the head. Shape pipe cleaner as shown in photo.

Tie white ribbon into a small bow. Glue bow below head.

Cut photo the size of angel's head with subject of photo centered. Apply a bead of glue to the back of pipe cleaner head. Center right side of photo on back of head. Let dry.

Glue magnetic strip centered on back of photo, or tie nylon thread to top of halo for hanger. ★

As You Take Down The Christmas Tree, Spruce Up Memories!

TRIMMING the Christmas tree is a treasured tradition with many families—but taking it down may not be! These tips can help you save time—and merry memories—for next year.

• Plan ahead to make an ornament from your Christmas tree! Before putting this year's tree in water, cut a small thin slice from the trunk. Let it dry until your tree comes down.

Then help your child sand the front smooth and decorate with paints and color markers or bits of Christmas fabrics and felt. After your little crafter adds his name and the year, form a hanging loop by gluing a piece of string to the top center back of the slice.

• When removing strings of tree lights, replace all burnt-out bulbs before putting them away.

• Save the boxes from new ornaments to use for storage another year.

• Label each box as you fill it with decorations. Be specific!

• When removing ornaments, use a needle-nose pliers to secure the hook in each. That way, says Joy Beck of Cincinnati, Ohio, you'll save time hunting for stray ornament hooks next year.

• As you dismantle the tree, ask family members for a fun prediction or resolution for the year ahead. Or make a note of each one's favorite holiday moment or memory this year. Then tuck the notes in with your ornaments and read them as you decorate next year's tree!

The Time's Right for Quick Cross-Stitch Cards

Finished Size: Card measures 5-1/2 inches high x 4-1/4 inches wide. The design area is 48 stitches high x 27 stitches wide and measures about 1-1/2 inches wide x 2-5/8 inches high.

Directions:
Zigzag or overcast edges of Aida cloth to prevent fraying. Fold Aida cloth in half lengthwise, then in half crosswise to find center and mark this point.

To find center of chart, draw lines across chart connecting opposite arrows. Begin stitching at this point so design will be centered.

Working with 18-in. lengths of six-strand floss, separate strands and use two strands for cross-stitching and one strand for French knot and backstitching. See Fig. 1 for stitch illustrations.

Each square on chart equals one stitch worked over a set of fabric threads. Use colors indicated on color key to complete cross-stitching, then backstitching.

Do not knot floss on back of work. Instead, leave a short tail of floss on back of work and hold in place while working the first few stitches over it. To end a strand, run needle under a few neighboring stitches in back before cutting floss close to work.

ASSEMBLY: With design centered, trim Aida cloth to a 4-in. x 5-in. piece.

Center cross-stitched design on inside of card behind oval window opening. Apply a thin bead of glue to Aida cloth near edges of window opening to attach design to card.

Glue white paper centered behind design area on inside of card. Let dry.

Make a bunch and mail to family and friends! ★

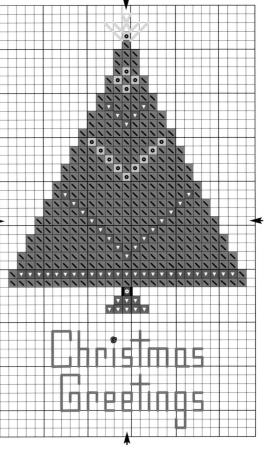

A SINGLE shining Christmas tree, designed in cross-stitch by Edna Lanners of Oakdale, Minnesota, posts the perfect season's greeting to her extra-special friends at the holidays.

"The cards work up so quickly—almost in less time than it takes to lick a stamp," Edna laughs. "A touch of gold thread turns them into shining keepsakes for next year's tree."

Materials Needed:
Chart above right
5-inch x 4-inch piece of off-white 18-count Aida cloth
Purchased 4-1/4-inch x 5-1/2-inch blank off-white card with 3-inch x 3-5/8-inch oval window opening and matching envelope
4-inch x 5-1/4-inch piece of white paper
DMC six-strand embroidery floss in colors listed on color key
Size 24 tapestry needle
White (tacky) glue
Scissors

CROSS-STITCHED CHRISTMAS TREE CARD	
COLOR KEY	**DMC**
▼ Bright Holiday Red	666
◣ Bright Holiday Green	700
⊙ Holiday Gold	783
⊡ Dark Coffee Brown	801
BACKSTITCHING	
— Bright Holiday Red	666
— Holiday Gold	783
▬ Dark Coffee Brown	801
FRENCH KNOT	
❀ Bright Holiday Red	666

Fig. 1

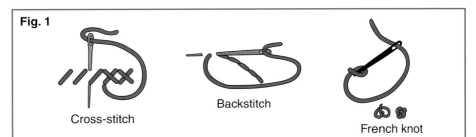

Cross-stitch

Backstitch

French knot

Jolly Elf Will Ho-Ho-Hold His Own on Any Shelf

THIS JAUNTY shelf-sitting Santa will make you laugh when you see him—in spite of yourself! Follow Louise Vaillancourt's simple directions to fashion your own version from a wood block, scraps of fabric, a little paint and snips of yarn.

"This Santa was a real hit with family, friends and my son's teacher last year," Louise writes from her home in Gatineau, Quebec.

Materials Needed:
Pattern on next page
Tracing paper and pencil
2-1/2-inch length of 2 x 4 pine for body (2 x 4 pine actually measures 1-1/2 inches x 3-1/2 inches)
1-1/2-inch wooden doll head
Drill with 1/2-inch bit
Sandpaper and tack cloth
Foam plate or palette
Paper towels
Container of water
Acrylic craft paints—dark pink, flesh, red and white
Paintbrushes—small flat, small round and 1-inch foam brush
18-inch square of large red-and-black plaid flannel or lightweight wool for hat, arms and legs
4-inch x 9-inch piece of white fleece for fur trim
Scrap of red felt for mouth
Two 3/8-inch black buttons
1/2-inch white pom-pom
White and black all-purpose thread
3-1/2 yards of white textured yarn for beard
Black fine-line permanent marker
Uncooked rice or plastic doll pellets
Measuring spoons—tablespoon and teaspoon
Clear varnish
White (tacky) glue
Standard sewing supplies

Finished Size:
Santa measures about 10 inches high x 8-1/2 inches wide.

Directions:
Referring to Fig. 1 for placement, drill a 1/2-in. hole through 1-1/2-in. side of pine wood piece 3/4 in. down from top for arms. Drill a 1/2-in. hole through 2-1/2-in. side of wood piece 3/4 in. from side and bottom edges for legs.

Sand wood surfaces to smooth. Wipe wood with tack cloth to remove dust from surface and from drilled holes.

Place small amounts of paint on foam plate or palette as needed. Paint as directed in instructions that follow, applying additional coats of paint as needed for complete coverage. Let paint dry after each application.

Using foam brush, paint entire wood piece red for body.

Apply one coat of varnish to wood block. Let dry.

Paint wood doll head flesh using flat brush.

From plaid fabric, cut a 4-1/2-in. x 16-in. piece for legs. Fold fabric strip in half lengthwise with right sides facing and edges matching. Sew long edges together with a 1/4-in. seam. Turn right side out.

Insert an end of leg piece through each drilled leg hole in body, centering piece so legs hang evenly in front.

Cut one 4-1/2-in. x 11-1/2-in. piece from plaid fabric for arms. Fold strip in half lengthwise with right sides facing. Sew long edges together with a 1/4-in. seam. Turn right side out.

Insert arms through drilled arm hole in body with ends hanging evenly at the sides.

Turn raw edges of legs and arms 5/8 in. to wrong side. Thread hand-sewing needle with black thread. Sew around arm and leg opening with a running stitch, leaving long thread ends on each. See Fig. 2 for stitch illustration.

Pour 1 tablespoon of uncooked rice or plastic doll pellets into a leg. Pull thread ends taut to close. Knot thread ends together and clip close to knot. Repeat for other leg.

Pour 1 teaspoon of uncooked rice or plastic doll pellets into each arm and close each as for legs.

Cut four 3/8-in. x 3-in. lengths of white fleece for arm and leg trims. Starting at each seam, glue a strip around end of each arm and leg, covering gathering thread. Trim excess.

Cut a 5/8-in. x 2-1/2-in. strip of fleece for jacket trim. Glue strip down the center front of body, ending strip 1-1/2 in. from the bottom.

Cut a 5/8-in. x 8-1/2-in. strip of fleece. Starting in back, glue strip around body above leg holes. Trim excess.

Glue buttons to jacket trim, referring to photo for placement.

Glue flat side of head centered on top of body.

Cut twenty-one 2-1/2-in.-long pieces of white yarn. Glue yarn to back and sides of head for hair. Trim hair as desired.

Cut seven 4-1/2-in.-long pieces of white yarn. Fold each piece in half. Referring to photo for placement, glue fold of each piece to head for beard, leaving space for facial features. Trim beard as desired.

Cut a 1-in. length of white yarn for mustache. Wrap white thread around middle of strand and knot to hold. Cut

threads close to knot. Glue mustache on top of center of beard.

Trace hat pattern onto tracing paper as directed on pattern. Cut hat from plaid fabric as directed on pattern.

Fold hat with right sides together and side edges matching. Sew sides together with a 1/4-in. seam. Turn hat right side out.

Glue hat to head with seam in back, covering ends of hair. Starting at the back, glue a 5/8-in.-wide strip of white fleece around hat, covering raw edge of hat. Trim excess.

Fold tip of hat down and to the side as shown in photo. Spot-glue as needed to hold. Glue pom-pom to tip of hat.

Cut a small oval from red felt for mouth. Glue mouth onto beard under mustache.

Using round brush, paint a dark pink oval above mustache for nose.

Mix a bit of white with dark pink to make light pink. Using a nearly dry flat brush, add light pink cheeks to face.

Use black marker to add two small dots for eyes.

Use round brush to add white eyebrows above eyes.

Perch your Santa on a mantel or special package!

Fig. 1 Drilling arm and leg holes in pine wood piece

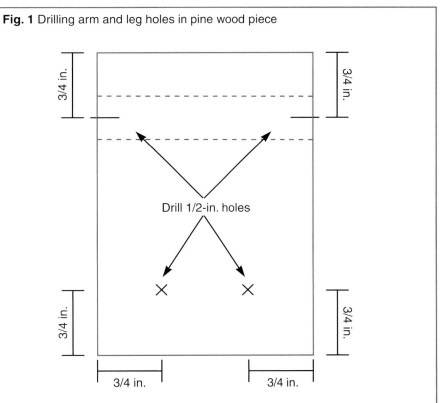

3/4 in.   3/4 in.

Drill 1/2-in. holes

3/4 in.   3/4 in.

3/4 in.   3/4 in.

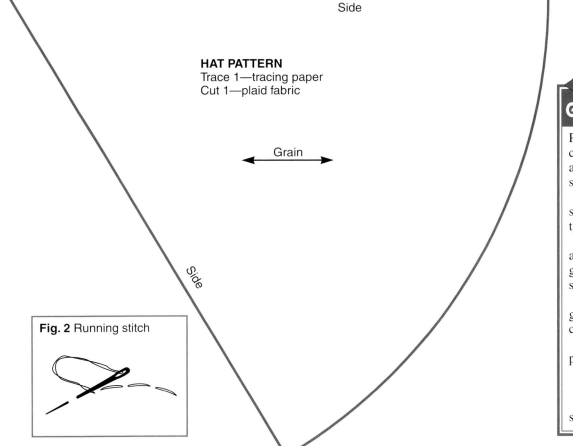

Side

HAT PATTERN
Trace 1—tracing paper
Cut 1—plaid fabric

Grain

Side

Fig. 2 Running stitch

Gift Wrapping Tips

PACKAGE TOPPERS can make your wrapping as special as the gift inside. Try adding:

❉ Bows made of bright shoelaces for boys or pretty hair ribbons for girls.

❉ Natural trims such as dried flowers, evergreen sprigs, pinecones or seashells.

❉ Tiny ornaments or gingerbread boys, cookie cutters or candy canes.

❉ Silk flowers or a pretty holiday corsage.

❉ Festive bookmarks.

❉ Colorful seed pack.

❉ Rolled up sheet music or a map or magazine.

Angel's a Reminder of Glad Tidings

HARK, this herald angel has cross-stitched wings spread wide to bring tidings of great joy! To fashion the seraph's skirt more quickly, crafter Renee Dent of Conrad, Montana simply glued fabric over a paper cone.

"Use her as a tree trim or a stand-alone figure," Renee suggests.

Materials Needed:
Pattern on next page
Chart below
Tracing paper and pencil
5-inch x 6-inch piece of white 14-count Aida cloth
5-inch x 6-inch piece of white felt
DMC six-strand embroidery floss in colors listed on color key
Size 24 tapestry needle
9-1/2-inch x 5-inch piece of white card stock or heavy paper
9-1/2-inch x 5-inch piece of green solid cotton or cotton-blend fabric for skirt
9-inch x 4-1/2-inch piece of paper-backed fusible web
Low-temperature glue gun and glue sticks
Iron and ironing surface
Seam sealant
Spring clothespin
Transparent tape
White (tacky) glue

Finished Size: Angel measures about 6 inches high x 4 inches across. Design area is 41 stitches high x 60 stitches wide and measures about 4-3/8 inches wide x 3 inches high.

Directions:
Zigzag or overcast edges of Aida cloth to prevent fraying. Fold Aida cloth in half lengthwise, then in half crosswise to determine center and mark this point.

To find center of chart, draw lines across chart connecting arrows. Begin stitching at this point so design will be centered.

Working with 18-in. lengths of six-strand floss, separate strands and use two strands for cross-stitching and one strand for backstitching. See Fig.1 for stitch illustrations.

Each square on chart equals one stitch worked over a set of fabric threads. Use colors indicated on color key to complete cross-stitching, then backstitching.

Do not knot floss on back of work. Instead, leave a short tail of floss on back of work and hold in place while working the first few stitches over it. To end a strand, run needle under a few neighboring stitches in back before cutting floss close to work.

With edges matching, glue felt to wrong side of finished cross-stitched

area with white glue. Let dry.

Cut out cross-stitched design, cutting one row outside stitching. Apply seam sealant to edges. Let dry.

Use copy machine to enlarge pattern to 200%, or mark tracing paper with a 1-in. grid and draw pattern as shown onto tracing paper.

Trace the skirt pattern onto folded tracing paper. Cut out and open for complete pattern.

Center fusible web on the wrong side of green solid fabric. Fuse in place following manufacturer's directions. Re-

CROSS-STITCHED CHRISTMAS ANGEL CHART

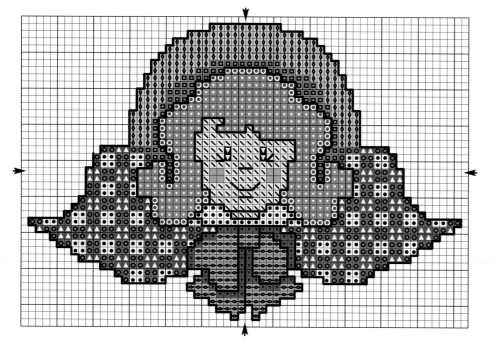

CROSS-STITCHED CHRISTMAS ANGEL COLOR KEY	DMC
⬤ White	000
⬛ Holiday Red	321
⊙ Medium Brown	433
◩ Light Holiday Green	701
⬛ Topaz	725
◆ Light Topaz	726
▽ Very Dark Topaz	780
◼ Garnet	816
◧ Very Light Sportsman Flesh	951
▼ Black Brown	3371
▲ Ultra Very Dark Emerald Green	3818
▨ Very Light Terra Cotta	3779
BACKSTITCHING	
— Black Brown	3371

move the paper backing and fuse to the white card stock or heavy paper with the edges matching.

Trace around skirt pattern onto card stock side of fused fabric. Cut out skirt, cutting just inside traced lines.

Wrap skirt into a cone shape, overlapping the side edges a bit. Glue overlapped edges with white glue. Use a clothespin to hold the edges together and transparent tape as needed to hold the top part where the clothespin cannot reach. When dry, remove the clothespin and tape.

Use low-temperature glue gun to glue the felt side of cross-stitched angel to top of skirt opposite the seam.

To use as a Christmas ornament, stitch a loop of white floss to back top of angel's head for hanger. Omit hanger to use angel as a freestanding Christmas decoration.

Set your angel out and watch holiday spirits soar! ★

Fig. 1

Cross-stitch

Backstitch

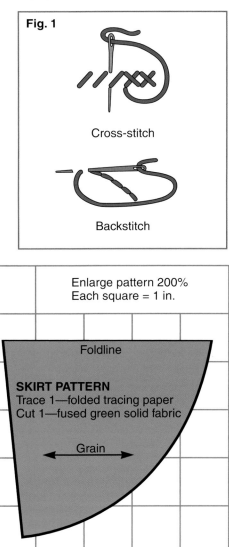

Enlarge pattern 200%
Each square = 1 in.

Foldline

SKIRT PATTERN
Trace 1—folded tracing paper
Cut 1—fused green solid fabric

Grain

Plant a Forest of Quick Cinnamon-Stick Trees

CREATE a grove of cinnamon-stick trees trimmed in homespun fabric and topped with stars! Yule find you can do it in a jiffy with bow-tied branches and simple directions from Sally Welter of Blaine, Minnesota.

So heat up the cider, put on some carols, and let the whole family share the fun of Christmas crafting as you harvest a stand of these pretty piney and so-easy ornaments.

Materials Needed (for one):
One 2-3/4-inch-long cinnamon stick
One 7/8-inch-high x 1/16-inch-thick
   purchased wooden star
Yellow acrylic craft paint
Small flat paintbrush
Iridescent glitter (optional)
2-inch x 2-1/2-inch piece of homespun
   or Christmas print fabric
7-inch length of natural 3-ply jute string
Ruler
Glue gun and glue stick
Scissors

Finished Size: Each ornament is about 3 inches high x 2 inches wide without hanger.

Directions:
Paint entire star yellow. If desired, sprinkle on iridescent glitter while paint is still wet. Let dry.

Glue star to flat side of one end of cinnamon stick.

Cut fabric into five 2-1/2-in.-long x 3/8-in.-wide strips. Tie an overhand knot in center of each strip of fabric.

With knots centered, trim ends of strips to make 1-in.-, 1-1/4-in.-, 1-1/2-in.-, 1-3/4-in.- and 2-in.-long strips.

With right sides of the strips facing the same direction, glue the knot of each strip along the length of the cinnamon stick, placing the first about 1/4 in. below the star and leaving about 1/2 in. of the cinnamon stick exposed for trunk as shown in photo above.

Fold jute string in half and glue ends together onto back of top of cinnamon stick for hanger.

Trim boughs with these beauties! ★

Season's Greetings Are Packed In Pretty Painted Planters

HOLLY TRIM and peppermint candies give this simple clay pot a festive flair to match the season. Designer Carol Brandon of Uxbridge, Ontario uses the painted pots to package Christmas plants, cookies or candies. "I also fill them with berries and greens to make a rustic centerpiece," she notes.

Materials Needed:

Two small pieces of household sponge
3-7/8-inch x 6-1/2-inch clay flowerpot
Water basin
Paper towels
Foam plate or palette
Paintbrushes—No. 6 flat, No. 8 flat and No. 1 script liner
Acrylic craft paints—Christmas Red, French Vanilla, Green Forest, Maple Syrup, School Bus Yellow, Taffy and Wicker White (Carol used Plaid FolkArt paints)
Acrylic varnish

Finished Size: Painted clay planter measures about 6-1/2 inches across x 3-7/8 inches high.

Directions:

PAINTING: Keep paper towels and a basin of water handy to clean brushes. Place dabs of each paint color onto palette or foam plate as needed. Let paint dry after each application unless instructions say otherwise.

Garland design is painted freehand, following Figs. 1-4 below. If desired, practice each paint stroke before painting the flowerpot. Refer to pattern and photo while painting as directed.

Flowerpot background: Use a dry piece of household sponge and Taffy to sponge-paint the entire clay pot, extending paint onto the edges, bottom and inside of the pot.

To sponge-paint, dip sponge into paint and then pounce sponge onto foam plate or palette to remove excess paint from sponge. Pounce sponge straight up and down on clay pot, making sure not to swirl sponge. Let some of the clay pot show through.

While Taffy paint is still wet, dip same sponge in French Vanilla and remove excess paint the same as before. Sponge on French Vanilla until Taffy is lightened to desired color, making both colors visible. Let dry.

Vines: Double-load No. 6 flat brush with Green Forest and School Bus Yellow by dipping one corner of brush into green and the other side into yellow. Work the brush back and forth on palette or foam plate until colors blend. Repeat three or four times in the same blending strip until the paint is three-fourths of the way up the brush bristles.

Referring to Fig. 1, use the chisel (thin) edge of brush to paint wavy, thin lines all the way around the pot, keeping brush handle upright and leading with School Bus Yellow. Pick up more paint on brush as needed.

Leaves: Leaves are painted with two strokes per leaf. Double-load No. 6 flat brush with Green Forest and School Bus Yellow. Pick up more paint on each edge of brush. Do not blend paint. Paint one side of the leaf by placing the brush near a vine and pressing it in a wavy line as you paint the first stroke. See Fig. 2a.

Pick up more paint on each side of brush and paint the other side of leaf, reversing the brush to keep the yellow paint in center of leaf as shown in Fig. 2b.

With same brush, add stem and a vein down the center of leaf using chisel edge of brush and leading with School Bus Yellow edge. See Fig. 2b.

Continue to paint all the leaves around the pot in the same way.

Candy: Load No. 8 flat brush with Wicker White and Maple Syrup, using three-quarters Wicker White and one-quarter Maple Syrup. With the Maple Syrup on the outside, turn the brush in a circle to basecoat a round candy piece. See Fig. 3a. Basecoat the remaining candy pieces in the same way.

Load No. 6 flat with Christmas Red. Referring to Fig. 3b, apply paint from the outside of the circle to center, turning brush so chisel (thin) edge of brush is at center of candy. Paint three stripes on each candy piece in this way.

Thin Wicker White with clean water to an ink-like consistency. Use script liner to add highlights to each candy piece as shown in Fig. 3c.

In same way, thin Green Forest. Use script liner to paint tendrils by adding thin curvy lines, starting at the vine and extending over leaves, and ending by lifting up on brush to leave a pointed end as shown in Fig. 4.

Use a damp household sponge piece and Green Forest to lightly sponge-paint the rim of the pot. Let dry. Following manufacturer's instructions, apply varnish to clay pot. Let dry. ★

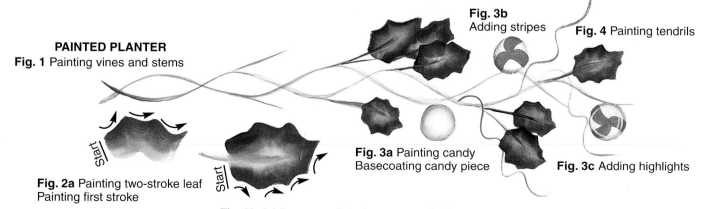

PAINTED PLANTER
Fig. 1 Painting vines and stems

Fig. 2a Painting two-stroke leaf
Painting first stroke

Start

Start

Fig. 2b Adding second stroke, stem and vein

Fig. 3a Painting candy
Basecoating candy piece

Fig. 3b Adding stripes

Fig. 3c Adding highlights

Fig. 4 Painting tendrils

Wreath Motif Sets Table in Festive Style

SHED SOME LIGHT on your Yule table with a bright two-tiered wooden wreath candle holder and matching napkin rings. The bright idea comes from Lana Condon of Jupiter, Florida, who includes easy-to-follow craft directions.

Materials Needed:
Purchased unfinished wooden wreath cutouts—two 7-3/4-inch-diameter x 3/16-inch-thick wreaths and six 3-inch-diameter x 3/16-inch-thick wreaths (see shopping information)
Three 1-1/4-inch-high wooden flowerpots
Eighteen 3/8-inch-diameter x 1/16-inch-thick wooden circles and twelve 1-1/4-inch-long x 1/16-inch-thick wooden diamond shapes (Lana used Woodsies)
Sandpaper and tack cloth
Three 20mm red wooden beads with 10mm holes or holes to fit candles
Three 4-inch-tall white candles (Lana used wind chime candles)
Foam plate or palette
Acrylic craft paints—green, red and white
Paintbrushes—1/2-inch flat and 1-inch foam
White (tacky) glue

Shopping Information: The precut scalloped wooden wreath pieces in both the 7-3/4-in. and 3-in. size are available from The Craft Basket, 117 Old State Rd., Brookfield CT 06804; or by phoning 1-203/740-2999.

Finished Size: Wreath candle holder measures about 7-3/4 inches in diameter x 2 inches high without candles. Each

wreath napkin ring measures about 3 inches across.

Directions:
Sand all wooden pieces smooth and wipe with tack cloth.

Place small amounts of paint on foam plate or palette as needed. Paint wood pieces as directed below. Add additional coats of paint as needed for complete coverage. Let paint dry after each application.

Use foam brush to paint the two 7-3/4-in. wreaths green and the six 3-in. wreaths white.

Use flat brush to paint the circles red and the diamonds green.

Use foam brush to paint the flowerpots red.

Glue inverted flowerpots to top of one 7-3/4-in. green wreath, spacing them evenly around the wreath as shown in photo above.

Glue remaining 7-3/4-in. green wreath to bottom of flowerpots, positioning second wreath identically above lower wreath. Let dry.

Referring to photo for position, glue three red circles onto one side of each of the 3-in. white wreaths for holly berries and two green diamonds below red circles for holly leaves. Let dry.

Referring to photo for position, glue the three white wreaths right side up and evenly spaced around top green wreath. Glue red beads between white wreaths with holes of beads facing up for candle holders. Let dry.

Use remaining wreaths as napkin rings at a festive gathering! ★

Decking the Halls Makes Merry Memories

"CHRISTMAS has always been a time of special rituals for my family," writes Ann McConnell, Abingdon, Virginia.

"One Yuletide tradition began when my daughters were 2 and 4 years old. Now 22 and 24, they still share this ritual with my mother, their 'Nana'.

"Thanksgiving weekend was a very busy time at my husband's parents' house. So when the girls were little,

my parents asked us to bring them to their house Thanksgiving night and let them spend the weekend.

"When my husband and I arrived to pick the girls up on Sunday afternoon, they couldn't wait to show us how they'd decorated their grandparents' house—from top to bottom—and using an abundance of tape!

"Over the years, a little brother was

added to the team. My mother made most of the ornaments the children used in their beautiful decorating. Each summer, Nana and her three decorators would begin planning what to do in all the different rooms.

"After my father died, this tradition came to mean even more to my mother, who is now 86.

"Today, some of the kids are out of college and have busy holiday schedules, but they still decorate with Nana."

Cozy Up to Christmas with Quilted Tea Set

Directions:

Pre-wash fabrics, washing each color separately. If water is discolored, wash again until rinse water runs clear. Dry and press all fabrics.

Cut all fabrics using rotary cutter and quilter's ruler, or mark fabrics using ruler and marker of choice and cut with scissors. Cut all strips crosswise from selvage to selvage.

Do all piecing with accurate 1/4-in. seams, right sides of fabrics together, edges matching and matching thread.

MINI QUILT: From green-on-white print, cut eighteen 2-in. squares, two 1-1/2-in. x 7-in. strips for tree blocks and six 3-in. squares for snowman blocks. Cut two 2-1/2-in. x 12-1/2-in. strips and two 2-1/2-in. x 18-1/2-in. strips for borders. Also cut one 1-1/2-in. x 12-1/2-in. strip for pieced corners and one 16-in. x 22-in. piece for backing.

From brown print, cut one 1-1/2-in. x 7-in. strip for tree trunks.

From green-and-white plaid, cut six 3-7/8-in. squares for snowman blocks.

From dark green print, cut nine 2-in. x 3-1/2-in. rectangles for tree blocks, one 1-1/2-in. x 12-1/2-in. strip for pieced corners and two 2-1/4-in. x 44-in. strips for binding.

From red snowman print, cut three 3-1/2-in. squares with snowman design centered for snowman blocks and six 2-in. x 6-1/2-in. strips for borders of tree blocks.

Tree block (make three): On wrong side of all green-on-white print 2-in. squares, mark a diagonal line with quilter's marking pen or pencil.

Sew a green-on-white print square to one end of dark green print 2-in. x 3-1/2-in. rectangle with edges matching as shown in Fig. 1. Stitch on marked line of green-on-white print square. Trim seam allowance to 1/4 in. from stitching. Open and press seam toward piece just added.

A CUP of Christmas tea has never been so merry! Steeped in down-home nostalgia, the patchwork pattern on this mini quilted table topper, tea cozy and hot pads pulls together holiday fabrics.

Designer Jeanne Prue of Newport, Vermont writes, "This set makes a lovely gift or a warm welcome for holiday visitors who come to call."

Materials Needed (for all):
All-purpose thread to match fabrics
Quilter's marking pen or pencil
Quilter's ruler
Rotary cutter and mat (optional)
Standard sewing supplies

Materials Needed (for mini quilt):
44-inch-wide 100% cotton or cotton-blend fabrics—3/4 yard of green-on-white print, 1/4 yard of green-and-white plaid, 1/4 yard of dark green print, 3/8 yard of red snowman print and scrap or 1/8 yard of brown print
18-inch x 24-inch piece of lightweight quilt batting

Materials Needed (for tea cozy):
44-inch-wide 100% cotton or cotton-blend fabrics—1/2 yard of green-on-white print, 1/8 yard of green-and-white plaid, 1/8 yard of dark green print, 1/8 yard of red snowman print and scrap or 1/8 yard of brown print
16-inch x 26-inch piece of lightweight quilt batting

Materials Needed (for two hot pads):
44-inch-wide 100% cotton or cotton-blend fabrics—1/8 yard of green-on-white print, 1/4 yard of green-and-white plaid, 1/8 yard of dark green print for border, 1/8 yard of red snowman print and scrap or 1/8 yard of brown print
Two 9-inch squares of cotton quilt batting

Finished Size: Mini quilt measures about 16-1/2 inches wide x 22-1/2 inches long. Tea cozy measures about 13 inches across x 7-1/2 inches high. Each hot pad measures about 8 inches square.

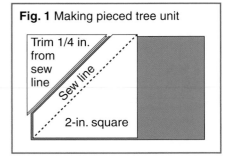

Fig. 1 Making pieced tree unit

Trim 1/4 in. from sew line

Sew line

2-in. square

In same way, sew another green-on-white print square to the opposite end of same dark green print rectangle to make a 2-in. x 3-1/2-in. pieced rectangle. See Fig. 2.

Fig. 2 Completed pieced tree unit

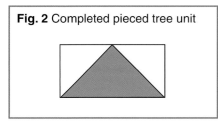

Lay out three pieced rectangles with right sides up as shown in Fig. 3. Sew the pieced rectangles together to make tree unit as shown. Press seams toward top of tree unit.

Fig. 3 Pieced tree unit

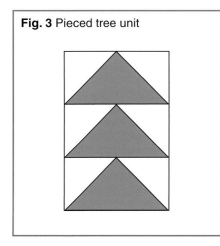

Sew a 1-1/2-in. x 7-in. green-on-white print strip to each long edge of the 1-1/2-in. x 7-in. brown print strip. Press seams toward darker fabric. Cut pieced strip into three 2-in. x 3-1/2-in. pieces for the trunk units. See Fig. 4.

Fig. 4 Cutting tree trunk units

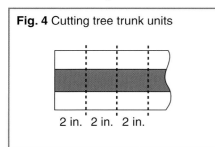

2 in. 2 in. 2 in.

Sew a tree trunk unit to bottom of each tree unit. Press seam toward tree trunk unit.

To complete the block, sew a red 2-in. x 6-1/2-in. strip to opposite sides of tree unit as shown in Fig. 5.

Repeat to make a total of three 6-1/2-in. square tree blocks.

Snowman block (make three): Cut two green-on-white print 3-in. squares in half diagonally to make four triangles. Sew the long edge of two triangles to opposite sides of a snowman square. Press seams away from center square.

Fig. 5 Completed tree block

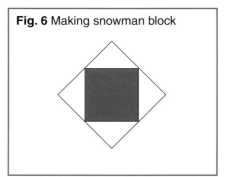

Then sew the long edge of the remaining triangles to the remaining opposite corners and press as before. See Fig. 6.

Fig. 6 Making snowman block

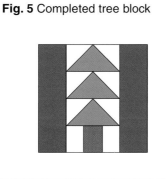

Cut two 3-7/8-in. green-and-white plaid squares in half diagonally to make two triangles. Then sew long edge of each triangle to opposite sides of pieced snowman square as before to make a pieced snowman block as shown in Fig. 7.

Fig. 7 Completed snowman block

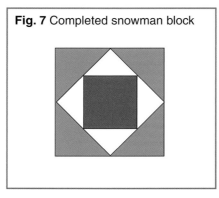

Repeat to make a total of three 6-1/2-in. square snowman blocks.

Four-patch corner (make four): Sew the long edges of a 1-1/2-in. x 12-1/2-in. dark green print strip and a 1-1/2-in. x 12-1/2-in. green-on-white print strip together. Press seam toward darker fabric. Cut strip into eight 1-1/2-in. x 2-1/2-in. pieced strips.

Sew two pieced strips together as shown in Fig. 8, carefully matching corners to make a four-patch corner. Repeat to make a total of 4 four-patched corners.

Fig. 8 Completed four-patch corner

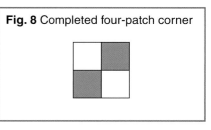

Quilt top assembly: Lay out the tree blocks and snowman blocks in three rows with two blocks in each row as shown in Fig. 9.

Fig. 9 Mini quilt top

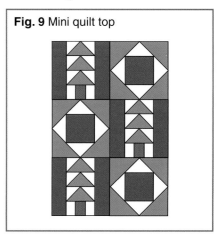

Sew the blocks in each row together as planned. Press seams in each row in opposite directions. Then sew the rows together, carefully matching all corners. Press seams open.

Border: Sew a 2-1/2-in. x 12-1/2-in. green-on-white print strip to the top and bottom edges of the pieced top. Press seams toward borders.

Sew a four-patch corner to each end of each 2-1/2-in. x 18-1/2-in. green-on-white print strip. Press seams toward borders.

Sew a pieced border to opposite sides of the quilt top, carefully matching corners. Press seams toward borders.

Quilting: Place backing fabric wrong side up on a flat surface. Place batting centered over backing and pieced top right side up on top of batting. Smooth out all layers.

Hand-baste all layers together, stitching from center to corners, then horizontally and vertically every 4 in.

(Continued on next page)

With white quilting thread, machine-stitch in-the-ditch of all seams. Also outline-stitch each border, stitching 1/4 in. from the seams. Stitch again 1/4 in. from that stitching, outlining the dark green squares in corners also.

Binding: Sew around outside, stitching 1/8 in. from edge of pieced top. Trim backing and batting even with pieced top.

Sew short ends of two 2-1/4-in. x 44-in. dark green print binding strips together to make one long strip. Cut one short end diagonally and press 1/4 in. to wrong side. Press strip in half lengthwise with wrong sides together.

With raw edges matching, stitch binding to right side of pieced top with a 1/4-in. seam, mitering corners.

Fold binding to the back of quilt, encasing raw edges, and hand-sew the fold to the back. Remove basting.

TEA COZY: From green-on-white print fabric, cut six 2-in. squares for tree block and two 3-in. squares for snowman block. Cut two 1-1/2-in. x 2-in. rectangles for trunk unit of tree block, and one 1-1/2-in. x 37-in. strip for pieced borders.

From brown print, cut one 1-1/2-in. x 2-in. rectangle for tree trunk.

From green-and-white plaid, cut two 3-7/8-in. squares for snowman block.

From dark green print, cut one 1-1/2-in. x 37-in. strip for pieced borders, three 2-in. x 3-1/2-in. rectangles for tree block and one 1-1/2-in. x 5-in. strip for top loop. Also cut four 1-1/2-in. x 13-1/2-in. strips for top and bottom borders.

From red snowman print, cut six 2-in. x 6-1/2-in. strips for borders and one 3-1/2-in. square with snowman centered for snowman block.

Following directions for tree quilt, make one tree block and one snowman block as shown in Figs. 5 and 7.

Checkerboard border (make four): Sew the long edges of the 1-1/2-in. x 37-in. dark green print strip and the 1-1/2-in. x 37-in. green-on-white strip together. Press seam toward darker fabric. Cut the strips into twenty-four 1-1/2-in. x 2-1/2-in. pieces.

Sew the long edges of six pieced strips together, carefully matching corners to make a 2-1/2-in. x 6-1/2-in. pieced checkerboard border as shown in Fig. 10. Repeat to make a total of four checkerboard borders.

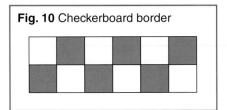

Fig. 10 Checkerboard border

Snowman side: Sew a checkerboard border to opposite sides of snowman block with long edges matching. Press seams toward snowman block.

Sew a 2-in. x 6-1/2-in. red snowman print border to each checkerboard border with long edges matching. Press seams toward snowman print border.

Sew a 1-1/2-in. x 13-1/2-in. dark green print border to top and bottom edges of pieced side. Press seams toward dark green print border.

Tree block side: Sew a checkerboard border to each red snowman print border of tree block with long edges matching. Press seams toward the tree block. Sew a red snowman print border to each checkerboard border with long edges matching. Press seams toward red snowman print border.

Sew a 1-1/2-in. x 13-1/2-in. dark green print border to top and bottom edges of pieced side. Press seams toward border.

Assembly: Round the upper corners of the tea cozy as shown in photo on page 80.

Using a pieced side for pattern, cut two pieces each of batting and lining.

Hand-baste batting to the wrong side of each pieced side.

For the top loop, fold the long edges of the 1-1/2-in. x 5-in. dark green print strip 1/4 in. to the wrong side. Fold strip in half lengthwise and topstitch close to the outer edge. Fold loop in half with raw edges together. Baste loop to the top center of one pieced side with raw edges matching.

Pin the two pieced sides together with right sides facing and edges matching and top loop between layers. Sew the pieced sides together with a 1/2-in. seam, stitching curved edge only.

Sew the curved edges of the two lining pieces together in the same way, leaving an opening for turning at the top.

Pin the lining and pieced tea cozy together with right sides facing and straight edges matching. Sew the straight edges together with a 1/2-in. seam.

Turn right side out through opening in lining. Hand-sew lining opening closed. Push lining into inside of tea cozy.

With dark green thread, topstitch 1/4 in. from the bottom (straight) edge.

With white thread, hand-quilt as desired. Remove basting.

HOT PADS: From green-on-white print, cut six 2-in. squares for tree block, two 3-in. squares for snowman block, and two 1-1/2-in. x 2-in. rectangles for trunk unit of tree block. Also cut two 8-1/2-in. squares for backing of hot pads.

From brown print, cut one 1-1/2-in. x 2-in. rectangle for tree trunk.

From green plaid, cut two 3-7/8-in. squares for snowman block.

From dark green print, cut three 2-in. x 3-1/2-in. rectangles for tree block. Cut four 1-1/2-in. x 6-1/2-in. strips and four 1-1/2-in. x 8-1/2-in. strips for borders. Cut two 1-1/2-in. x 3-in. strips for hanging loops.

From red snowman print, cut two 2-in. x 6-1/2-in. strips for border of tree block and one 3-1/2-in. square with snowman centered for snowman block.

Following directions for tree quilt, make one tree block as shown in Fig. 5 and one snowman block as shown in Fig. 7.

Sew a 1-1/2-in. x 6-1/2-in. dark green border to the top and bottom of the tree and snowman blocks. Press seams toward border.

Sew a 1-1/2-in. x 8-1/2-in. dark green border strip to the opposite sides of each block to make the fronts of each hot pad.

Stitch the two 1-1/2-in. x 3-in. strips for hanging loops as directed for the top loop of tea cozy. Baste a hanging loop to right side of upper right corner of each hot pad with raw edges matching.

Baste a pieced block centered right side up to each piece of batting.

Place a backing piece on top of each pieced block with right sides together and raw edges matching.

Sew each hot pad together, stitching 1/4 in. from edges of pieced blocks and leaving an opening for turning on one side.

Trim all layers, leaving a 1/4-in. seam allowance. Clip corners diagonally. Turn each hot pad right side out through opening. Turn raw edges of openings in and hand-sew openings closed.

With matching thread, stitch in-the-ditch of all seams on each hot pad. Remove all basting.

Invite guests to a holiday tea soon so you can use your new ensemble! ★

Quilting Tips

• If your cotton thread breaks frequently, put it in a plastic bag in the freezer. Remove after a few days. The thread will take on moisture as it thaws, restoring flexibility.

• To check accuracy of a 1/4-in. seam allowance, cut three 6-in. x 1-1/2-in. fabric strips. Sew together with a standard 1/4-in. seam; press open. With right sides facing, the width of the middle strip should be exactly 1 in. wide.

Tasteful Treats Are in the Bag!

GIFTS of homemade Christmas cookies will be savored down to the last buttery crumb—especially when wrapped in Alise Duerr's whimsical finery.

The clever crafter from Merritt Island, Florida shows how to "doll up" a plain brown paper bag in spicy, homespun touches for your presents from the pantry.

Materials Needed:
Pattern below
Tracing paper and pencil
6-inch x 9-inch brown paper gift bag with handles
Water basin
Paper towels
Foam plate or palette
Acrylic craft paints—black, burnt sienna, mocha, red and white
Paintbrushes—small flat, small round, liner and stencil brush
1/2-inch square checkerboard stencil
Old scruffy brush or toothbrush
Newspapers
23-inch x 1-1/4-inch torn strip of red-and-white plaid fabric

Finished Size: Gift bag measures 13 inches high x 6-1/2 inches wide x 3 inches deep, including handle.

Directions:
Place small amounts of paint on foam plate or palette as needed. Paint as directed.

Place checkerboard stencil pattern on front of gift bag about 1/4 in. from bottom edge. Use red and a nearly dry stencil brush to stencil squares with an up-and-down motion. Clean stencil. When dry, position stencil one square to the side and add white squares in the same way. Let dry.

Trace pattern onto tracing paper. Turn traced pattern over and rub flat side of pencil lead over traced lines to darken. Turn pattern right side up and center it on bag front about 1/2 in. above checkerboard. Retrace design lines with a dull pencil, transferring design onto bag.

Use flat brush and mocha to paint the gingerbread man.

Dip flat brush into clean water. Touch the brush to a paper towel so brush is wet but not dripping wet. Touch longer

corner of the brush into burnt sienna, then stroke the brush on a clean area of palette or foam plate to blend the paint and water. The color should fade from dark to light to clear.

Use to shade gingerbread man along the inner arms and upper legs to separate arms and legs from body. Shade the outside edge of arms and legs and the outer edge of head and body in the same way.

Use round brush and red to paint bow tie. Let dry.

Use round brush and black to paint buttons and eyes, nose and mouth. Let dry.

Dip toothpick in white and use to dab a tiny white dot on buttons, eyes, nose and mouth.

Use liner and white to paint icing lines on arms, legs and body.

Use liner and black to outline bow tie. Use liner and black to paint lettering.

Place bag on newspapers to protect work surface.

Thin white with clean water to an ink-like consistency. Dip scruffy brush or toothbrush into thinned paint. Aim brush toward bag and draw a paintbrush handle or your finger across bristles and lightly spatter front of bag.

Wrap fabric strip around handle of gift bag and tie in a bow. Trim ends at an angle.

Fill with cookies and give to a friend!

COOKIES FOR YOU GIFT BAG PATTERN
Trace 1—tracing paper
Paint as instructed in directions

Fun's A-Foot with Crazy-Quilt Stocking

SANTA will have more trouble filling this giant stocking with goodies than you will stitching it up! The nifty, thrifty idea was created by Theresa Mahl of Lawrenceburg, Kentucky.

"It's a great way to use up years of accumulated Christmas scrap material," she says. And oh, the memories that stocking will hold!

Materials Needed:
Pattern below
Tracing paper and pencil
Scraps of 100% cotton or cotton-blend coordinating fabrics (Theresa used 13 different fabrics)
Two 12-inch x 21-inch pieces of muslin for backing
2/3 yard of 44-inch-wide red solid 100% cotton or cotton-blend fabric for lining
8-inch x 20-inch piece of off-white fleece or robe velour for cuff and hanger
20-inch length of 1-inch-wide green-and-gold metallic braid or ribbon for trim
All-purpose thread to match fabrics
Rotary cutter and mat (optional)
Quilter's marking pen or pencil
Quilter's ruler
Standard sewing supplies

Finished Size: Stocking measures about 20 inches high x 10 inches wide.

Directions: Use copy machine to enlarge pattern below to 400%, or mark tracing paper with a 1-in. grid and draw pattern as shown onto tracing paper. Set pattern aside.

CRAZY QUILTING: Cut fabrics of varying sizes and shapes with straight edges, using rotary cutter and quilter's ruler, or mark fabrics using ruler and marker of choice and cut with scissors.

Place a fabric scrap in middle of one muslin backing piece and sew 1/8 in. from all edges. See Fig. 1.

Place another scrap, right side down, on top of first piece with raw edges matching along one edge. Sew through all layers as shown in Fig. 2, stitching 1/4 in. from raw edges. Turn second piece right side up and press.

Trim the edges of second scrap even with first scrap as shown in Fig. 3.

Add a third scrap as shown in Fig. 4. Turn piece right side up, press and trim.

Continuing in this way, add different scraps until the muslin backing is covered, making sure to vary colors, shapes and sizes of the fabric scraps. Trim the fabric scraps even with the outside edges of muslin backing.

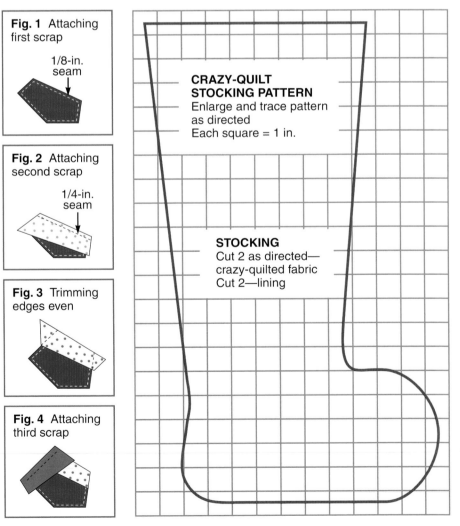

Fig. 1 Attaching first scrap

1/8-in. seam

Fig. 2 Attaching second scrap

1/4-in. seam

Fig. 3 Trimming edges even

Fig. 4 Attaching third scrap

CRAZY-QUILT STOCKING PATTERN
Enlarge and trace pattern as directed
Each square = 1 in.

STOCKING
Cut 2 as directed—crazy-quilted fabric
Cut 2—lining

Repeat on other muslin piece.

CUTTING: Layer both pieced fabrics with wrong sides together and edges matching. Pin stocking pattern to layered fabrics and cut out stocking on traced pattern lines.

Fold lining fabric in half with right sides together. Place stocking pattern on top and cut out stocking lining.

From fleece or robe velour fabric, cut a 6-in. x 18-1/2-in. piece for cuff and a 2-in. x 10-in. piece for hanging loop.

ASSEMBLY: With right sides together and raw edges matching, sew stocking pieces together, leaving top open. Clip curves and turn right side out.

In same way, sew lining pieces together. Clip curves.

Pin trim for cuff to right side of 6-in. x 18-1/2-in. piece of cuff fabric, placing long edge of trim 1-1/2 in. from one long edge of cuff fabric. Hand-sew trim in place. Trim ends even with short ends of cuff fabric.

With the right sides together and edges matching, sew short edges of the cuff together.

Fold cuff in half lengthwise with wrong sides together and raw edges matching.

Fold 2-in. x 10-in. fabric piece for hanging loop in half lengthwise with right sides together. Sew long edges together with a narrow seam, leaving ends open. Turn right side out.

Place lining inside stocking with wrong sides together.

Baste raw edges of hanging loop to lining side at back seam.

Pin folded cuff to lining side with trim side facing lining and raw edges of cuff, lining, stocking and loops matching. Sew around top through all layers with a 3/8-in. seam. Pull cuff up and press seam allowance toward stocking. Sew around top 1/4 in. from seam, stitching through stocking, lining and seam allowance. Turn cuff down. ★

Cute Critters Celebrate Christmas

MOOOVE OVER, Rudolph! No matter how crowded your Christmas tree, you'll want to make room for a herd of these frisky lightbulb cows! "They're a fun and easy family project," writes ornament crafter Michelle Mauk of Plymouth, Wisconsin.

Using throw-away, burned-out bulbs, this "bright" idea also makes a thrifty gift for teachers or unexpected guests.

Materials Needed:

Patterns below
Tracing paper and pencil
Standard lightbulb
Acrylic craft paints—black, pink, red and white
Flat white spray paint
Acrylic spray sealer
Black opaque paint pen
Felt—3-inch x 5-inch piece of black and 2-inch x 4-inch piece of pink for ears
Small flat paintbrush
Foam plate or palette

Two cotton balls
1/2-inch white pom-pom
12-inch length of 1/8-inch-wide gold braid or ribbon for hanger
White (tacky) glue
Two clothespins
Scissors

Finished Size: Lightbulb cow measures about 3-1/2-inches wide x 5 inches high without hanger.

Directions:

Spray lightbulb white following paint manufacturer's instructions. Let dry.

Place small amounts of paint onto foam plate or palette as needed. Paint as directed, applying additional coats as needed for complete coverage. Let paint dry after each application.

Paint metal base of lightbulb red.

Referring to painting diagram below, use pencil to draw face on lightbulb freehand.

Paint nose pink and mouth red.

Outline nose, eyes and mouth with black paint pen. Fill in eyes with black paint pen.

Dip end of paintbrush handle into white and use to dab a dot on eye.

Spray sealer on cow face only, following manufacturer's instructions.

Paint a few random black spots on lightbulb.

Trace ear patterns onto tracing paper. Cut out each on traced lines. Cut two black ears and two pink ears from felt.

Glue a pink felt ear onto center of each black felt ear with straight edges even. Fold each ear in half lengthwise with pink felt inside and glue straight ends together. Use clothespins to hold glued edges together until dry.

Referring to photo for placement, glue ears to lightbulb just below edge of red base on each side of face.

Wrap gold braid or ribbon around red base and knot in back. Knot ends together to form a hanger.

Stretch and glue cotton balls around bottom of red base for fur trim of hat, making sure cotton covers the ends of the ears and the ribbon or braid.

Glue pom-pom to top of hat. ★

LIGHTBULB COW PATTERNS

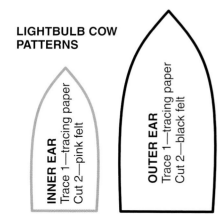

INNER EAR
Trace 1—tracing paper
Cut 2—pink felt

OUTER EAR
Trace 1—tracing paper
Cut 2—black felt

PAINTING DIAGRAM

Patchwork Piece Brings Heart to the Holidays!

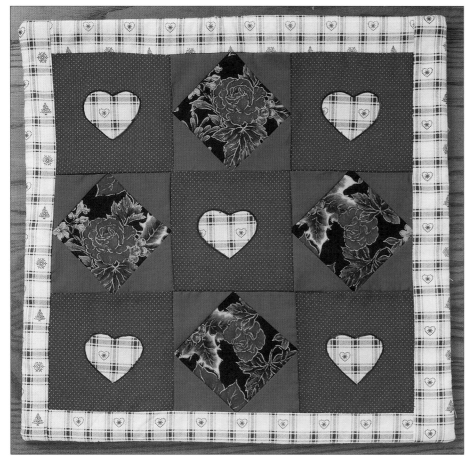

CHRISTMAS comes together in a heart-warming way with this handsome patchwork wall hanging designed by Loretta Kemna.

The skilled seamstress from St. Elizabeth, Missouri provides easy-to-follow directions for a bright banner that will create a comfy-cozy spot in whatever corner it hangs.

Materials Needed:
Pattern on next page
Pencil
44-inch-wide 100% cotton or cotton-blend fabrics—1/4 yard each of large Christmas print for pieced blocks, green solid for pieced blocks, red pin-dot for appliqued blocks and light Christmas print or plaid for heart appliques and border, and 3/4 yard of unbleached muslin for backing and hanging sleeve.
All-purpose thread to match fabrics
No-sew paper-backed fusible web for heart appliques

22-inch square of lightweight quilt batting
Rotary cutter and mat (optional)
Quilter's marking pen or pencil (optional)
Quilter's ruler
Black fine-line permanent marker
Standard sewing supplies
16-inch length of 1/4-inch wooden dowel

Finished Size: Wall hanging is about 18 inches square.

Directions:
CUTTING: Cut fabrics using rotary cutter and quilter's ruler, or mark fabrics using ruler and marker of choice and cut with scissors. Cut strips crosswise from selvage to selvage.

From large Christmas print, cut four 4-in. squares.

From red pin-dot, cut five 5-1/2-in. squares.

From green solid, cut eight 3-1/2-in. squares.

From light Christmas print or plaid,

cut two 2-in. x 15-1/2-in. strips and two 2-in. x 18-1/2-in. strips for borders.

From unbleached muslin, cut a 19-in. square for backing and a 2-in. x 17-in. strip for hanging sleeve.

APPLIQUED BLOCKS: Trace pattern onto paper side of fusible web as directed on pattern, leaving 1/2 in. between shapes. Cut shapes apart.

With grain lines matching, fuse hearts onto wrong side of light Christmas print or plaid fabric following manufacturer's directions. Cut out each heart on traced lines.

Remove paper backing and center each heart on right side of a red pin-dot square of fabric. Fuse each in place.

Outline each heart with black marker.

PIECING: Do all piecing with accurate 1/4-in. seams, right sides of fabrics together, edges matching and matching thread.

Cut each 3-1/2-in. green solid square in half diagonally to make 16 triangles. Sew the long edge of two green solid triangles to opposite sides of a 4-in. large Christmas print square. Press seams away from center square.

In the same way, add green solid triangles to remaining two sides of square. See Fig. 1. Trim the pieced block evenly to make an accurate 5-1/2-in. square. Repeat to make four 5-1/2-in. pieced blocks.

Fig. 1 Making pieced square

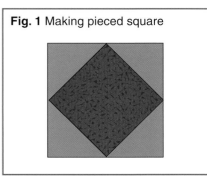

Lay out pieced blocks and appliqued blocks in three rows with three blocks in each row as shown in photo above left. Sew the blocks in each row together as planned. Press seams toward pieced squares.

Sew rows together, making sure all hearts face the same direction and carefully matching corners. Press seams open.

BORDER: Sew a 15-1/2-in.-long border strip to top and bottom edges of wall hanging. Press seams toward borders.

Sew an 18-1/2-in.-long border strip to

opposite sides of wall hanging and press seams as before.

QUILTING: Place batting on a flat surface. Center backing fabric right side up on top of batting and pieced wall hanging wrong side up on top of backing. Smooth out wrinkles and pin to hold.

Sew around outside of pieced wall hanging with a 1/4-in. seam, leaving an opening on one side for turning. Trim the excess batting and backing even with pieced top. Clip the corners diagonally.

Turn wall hanging right side out through opening with batting in the middle. Turn raw edges of opening in and hand-sew opening closed.

Hand- or machine-stitch in-the-ditch of all seams.

HANGING SLEEVE: Fold 1/4 in. twice to wrong side on each short edge of 2-in. x 17-in. muslin strip for hem.

Fold strip in half lengthwise with right sides together. Sew the long edges together. Turn right side out through opening at one end. Center seam and press.

Pin hanging sleeve centered along top edge on back of wall hanging. Hand-sew top and bottom folds of hanging sleeve to back of wall hanging, stitching through backing only.

Insert wooden dowel into hanging sleeve.

Hang your pretty patchwork piece and showcase for the holidays! ★

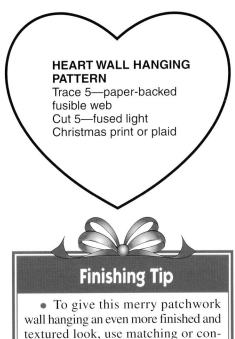

HEART WALL HANGING PATTERN

Trace 5—paper-backed fusible web
Cut 5—fused light
Christmas print or plaid

Finishing Tip

● To give this merry patchwork wall hanging an even more finished and textured look, use matching or contrasting thread to blanket stitch or satin stitch around all the heart appliques.

Cheery Crochet's a Pretty Way To Top Off Sweet 'Goodie' Jars

JUST TRY keeping the lid on this sweet idea from Doni Speigle of Claypool, Indiana! "It's one gift that's as good as it looks," Doni promises.

After dressing up canning jars with crocheted toppers, Doni fills them to the brim with red-and-white peppermints, striped ribbon candy or other old-time favorites for folks on her Christmas list.

Materials Needed:
Heavy-weight crochet cotton—small amount each of red and white (Doni used Aunt Lydia's Denim Quick Crochet)
Size E/4 (3.5mm) crochet hook or size needed to obtain correct gauge
Tapestry needle
Scissors
1-quart glass jar with lid
Peppermint candy to fill jar

Gauge:
End of Round 3 = 3 inches across.

Finished Size: Jar topper measures about 5 inches across.

Directions: With white, ch 4, join with a sl st to form a ring.

Round 1: Ch 3 (counts as first dc throughout), work 11 dcs in ring, join with a sl st in third ch of beginning ch-3: 12 dcs.

Round 2: Ch 3 and change to red when making third chain (do not fasten off white), dc in back lp of same st as joining, * pick up white and dc in back lp of next dc, pick up red and dc in back lp of same dc; repeat from * around, pick up white after last dc, join with a sl st in third ch of beginning ch-3: 24 dcs. Fasten off red.

Round 3: With white, ch 3, dc in same st, work 2 dcs in each dc around, join with a sl st in third ch of beginning ch-3: 48 dcs.

Round 4: Ch 3, dc in back lp of next dc and in back lp of each remaining dc around, join with a sl st in third ch of beginning ch-3: 48 dcs.

Round 5: Ch 4, sk next dc, dc in next dc, ch 1, * sk next dc, dc in next dc, ch 1; repeat from * around, attach red after last st, join with a sl st in third ch of beginning ch-4: 24 dcs and 24 ch-1 sps.

Round 6: With red, ch 1, sc in same

st as joining, sc in each dc and in each ch-1 sp around, pick up white after last st, join with a sl st in beginning sc: 48 scs.

Round 7: With white, ch 1, sc in same st as joining, * sk next sc, sc in next sc (dc with white, dc with red, dc with white, ch 2 with white, dc with white, dc with red, dc with white) for shell, sk next sc, sc in next sc; repeat from * around, join with a sl st in beginning sc: 12 shells and 12 scs. Fasten off.

Use yarn or tapestry needle to weave in all loose ends.

Jar Topper Cord: Working with a strand of red and white together as one, ch 100. Fasten off and weave in loose ends.

Weave cord through Round 5 of jar topper.

Fill jar with Christmas candies.

Place topper on jar lid. Tie ends of cord in a bow to secure topper on jar. ★

ABBREVIATIONS	
ch(s)	chain(s)
dc(s)	double crochet(s)
lp(s)	loop(s)
sc(s)	single crochet(s)
sl st	slip stitch
sp(s)	space(s)
sk	skip
st(s)	stitch(es)
( )	Instructions in parentheses are all worked in one stitch or space as indicated.
*	Instructions following an asterisk are repeated as directed.

Tot-Sized Apron Cooks Up in a Jingle!

THE SUGAR and spice and everything nice in Christmas cookies isn't quite as nice when it gets all over your tiniest kitchen helper. That's why you'll want to stitch up this cheery mini-apron designed by Darlene Polachic of Saskatoon, Saskatchewan.

Kids are sure to love the tree design Darlene appliqued, plus the button and jingle bell accents.

Materials Needed:
Pattern on next page
Tracing paper and pencil
100% cotton or cotton-blend fabrics—
   16-inch square of red solid for
   apron and 9-inch x 11-inch piece of
   green solid for tree applique
Quilter's marking pen or pencil
Two 36-inch lengths of red double-fold
   bias tape
Red all-purpose thread
8-1/2-inch x 10-1/2-inch piece of plas-
tic-coated freezer paper
Black six-strand embroidery floss
Embroidery needle
3/8-inch gold jingle bell
Buttons—two 5/8-inch yellow and two
   1/2-inch red
Standard sewing supplies

Finished Size: Apron measures about 15 inches long x 15 inches wide, excluding ties.

Directions:
Pre-wash fabrics without fabric softeners, washing each color separately. If water is discolored, wash again until rinse water runs clear. Dry and press fabrics.

Fold red solid fabric in half with wrong sides together.

Referring to Fig. 1 on next page and with fold of fabric on your right, mark top edge of apron 4 in. from fold and left edge 10 in. from bottom. Using quilt-

---

Put a Little Christmas in the Air

THE WONDERFUL AROMAS of Christmas can fill your home throughout the holiday season—even when you're not busy baking Christmas cookies and holiday treats, notes Peggy Key of Grant, Alabama.

Below, she shares a merry medley of spicy mixes, homemade potpourri recipes and tips for keeping the heartwarming and nostalgic scents of Christmas in the air at your house.

● For a spicy aroma in every nook and cranny of your house, try this: On a square of cheesecloth, combine 4 teaspoons whole allspice, 2 teaspoons whole cloves and 1 whole nutmeg. Add 2 cinnamon sticks. Gather the sides of the cheesecloth to form a packet and tie closed with a piece of string. Place the packet in a pot with 3 cups of wa-

ter. Bring water to a boil; reduce heat and let simmer.

● Bake orange and apple peels on a baking sheet at 200° until dry (about 4 to 5 hours). Mix the dry peels with crushed cinnamon sticks, whole nutmeg and a few whole cloves. Set out in pretty Christmas bowls. The aroma will remind you of gingerbread men baking in the oven!

● To brew a warm welcoming scent, pour 2 cups pineapple juice into a small saucepan. Add a few cinnamon sticks and a tablespoon of whole cloves, ground ginger or pickling spice. Bring the mixture to a boil, then reduce heat to low and simmer uncovered.

You can reuse this mix throughout the holidays by adding more water as liquid evaporates and reheating.

● For a quick, citrusy scent, mix 3 cups of water with the peel of an orange, lemon or apple and a few whole cloves or allspice. Bring the mixture to a boil and let the fresh fragrance permeate your kitchen.

● Spice up a batch of store-bought potpourri with a few cinnamon sticks or cloves. Put in a pretty basket or holiday Christmas bowl…and place in your bath or guest room.

● Here's a way to savor the fragrance of roses long after your blooms are gone. Dry the petals as soon as they start to wilt. Add some dried orange and lemon peel, cinnamon sticks broken into small pieces and whole cloves. Then mix in a teaspoon of orrisroot powder (available from The Spice House at *www.thespicehouse.com* or by calling 1-414/272-0977).

APPEALING AROMAS. *What special scent wafts through your house at Christmas? Share your secret recipe…and we might publish it in a future book! Send to "Potpourri, Country Woman Christmas, 5925 Country Lane, Greendale WI 53129".* ❉

er's marking pen or pencil, connect these marks with a curved line and cut along the line through both layers. Unfold apron.

Fold 1/4 in. twice to wrong side along top edge of apron. Sew close to first fold to hem. In same way, hem straight edges of sides and bottom of apron.

Pin a length of bias tape centered along the curved edge of each side of apron, encasing raw edge. Topstitch bias tape in place, extending stitching to sew folded edges of bias tape together.

Trace tree pattern onto folded tracing paper. Cut out on traced lines and open for a complete pattern.

Trace around tree pattern onto paper side of freezer paper. Cut out tree on traced lines.

Center freezer paper tree pattern onto wrong side of green solid fabric with grain lines matching. With an up-and-down motion, press plastic-coated side of freezer paper to wrong side of green solid fabric until freezer paper is lightly adhered to fabric.

Cut out tree, leaving a 1/4-in. margin of fabric around entire tree. Press margin of fabric snugly over the edge of the pattern to paper side of pattern. Carefully remove freezer paper pattern.

Pin tree applique right side up on front of apron as shown in photo.

Separate six-strand floss and thread embroidery needle with two strands. Blanket-stitch around edges of tree. See Fig. 2 for stitch illustration.

Sew jingle bell to top of tree and buttons down front of tree as shown in photo—and get your tot cookin'! ★

Fig. 2

Blanket stitch

TREE PATTERN
Trace 1—folded tracing paper
Cut 1 as directed—green solid

Grain

Foldline

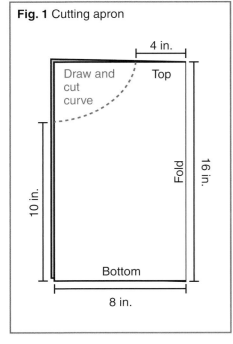

Fig. 1 Cutting apron

4 in.

Draw and cut curve

Top

10 in.

Fold

16 in.

Bottom

8 in.

She Sends Season's Greetings With Her Delightful Tree Trims

LIGHT AS A SNOWFLAKE, this jolly holiday duo is sure to brighten any tree or gift package—and couldn't be easier to whip up!

"It takes about 15 minutes to make either the Santa or the angel," explains Apollo, Pennsylvania crafter Sandy Rollinger, who sends the fun ornaments to her neighbors and friends instead of Christmas cards.

Materials Needed (for Santa and angel):

Patterns on next page
Tracing paper and pencil
Ballpoint pen
Scrap of lightweight cardboard
Glue stick
Powdered cosmetic blush
Cotton swab
Low-temperature glue gun and glue sticks
Two 8-inch lengths of silver thread for hangers
Scissors

Materials Needed (for Santa):

Craft foam—scraps each of flesh, red and white
Dimensional craft paints—red, green and crystal sparkle
Two 10mm glue-on wiggle eyes
3/8-inch white pom-pom
Decorative-edge scissors—optional (Sandy used Fiskars Cloud Paper Edgers)
1/4-inch round paper punch

Materials Needed (for angel):

Craft foam—scraps each of blue, flesh, red and white
Dimensional craft paints—black, gold, red and crystal sparkle
1-inch gold filigree circle for halo
Decorative-edge scissors—optional (Sandy used Fiskars Cloud and Victorian Paper Edgers)
1/2-inch clear faceted heart bead or novelty button

Finished Size: Santa measures about 4 inches across x 5-1/2 inches tall without hanger. Angel measures about 3-1/4 inches across x 4-1/2 inches tall without hanger.

Directions:

Trace patterns including dashed lines onto tracing paper with pencil. Use glue stick to glue patterns onto cardboard. Cut out patterns on traced lines.

Trace around patterns onto craft foam with ballpoint pen as directed on patterns. Cut out shapes, cutting just inside traced lines.

SANTA: Using regular scissors, trim edges of hat brim and both beard sections in a wavy pattern...or use Cloud decorative-edge scissors to trim edges.

Referring to pattern and photo for placement, glue hat brim onto bottom of hat and face onto hat brim.

Use cotton swab and a circular motion to apply powdered blush to cheeks.

Referring to pattern and photo for placement, glue small beard section onto large beard section and mustache to small beard. Glue beard onto face.

Use paper punch to cut nose from flesh craft foam. Glue the nose onto mustache and the eyes onto face above mustache.

Referring to photo for placement, use red dimensional paint to add a red dot for mouth below mustache.

Glue pom-pom to tip of hat.

Use green dimensional paint to add holly leaves to hat brim as shown in photo. When dry, use red dimensional paint to add berries to holly. Let dry.

Use crystal sparkle dimensional paint to add thin squiggly lines to mustache, on hat brim and beard and to add thicker lines for eyebrows. Let dry.

Knot ends of 8-in. length of silver thread together and glue to the back of the hat for hanger.

ANGEL: Using regular scissors, trim bottom edge of red, white and blue dress sections with a wavy pattern…or use Victorian decorative-edge scissors to trim edges.

Using regular scissors, trim bottom edge of wings with a wavy pattern…or use Cloud decorative-edge scissors to trim edge.

Referring to pattern for placement, glue red dress piece to white dress piece and blue dress piece to red dress piece, matching top and side edges of all pieces. Glue head to top of dress.

Use cotton swab and a circular motion to apply powdered blush to head.

Use black dimensional paint to add two small dots for eyes. Draw mouth with red dimensional paint. Let dry.

Use crystal sparkle dimensional paint to add thin squiggly lines to dress and wings. Let dry.

Glue heart bead or button onto dress.

Use gold dimensional paint to add hair to head. Let dry.

Glue halo to back of head and wings to back of dress.

Knot ends of an 8-in. length of silver thread together. Glue knot to back of head for hanger.

Hang Santa and angel ornaments on your Christmas tree. ★

SANTA AND ANGEL FOAM ORNAMENT PATTERNS

Trace 1 each piece—tracing paper
Cut 1 each piece—color of craft foam shown
on patterns

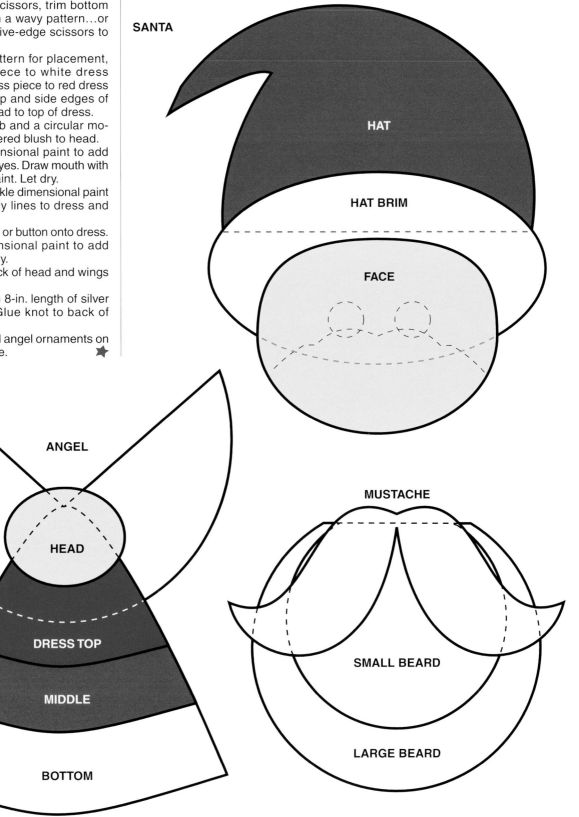

SANTA

HAT

HAT BRIM

FACE

ANGEL

WINGS

HEAD

DRESS TOP

MIDDLE

BOTTOM

MUSTACHE

SMALL BEARD

LARGE BEARD

Holiday Shirt Lights Up With Warm Family Feeling

BRIGHT BULBS and family names spell out the merry message—"You light up my life"—on this sew-easy holiday sweatshirt.

Designer Deborah Devine of Middleburgh, New York offers complete instructions for stitching the appliques, ruffled neckline and cuffs.

"To speed things up, you can attach the appliques to the sweatshirt with no-sew fusible web, then outline the lightbulbs with dimensional fabric paint," Deborah suggests.

Materials Needed:
Patterns at right and on next page
Tracing paper and pencil
White sweatshirt
100% cotton or cotton-blend fabrics—
12-inch x 15-inch piece of green pin-dot for tree; 3-inch square of brown solid for tree trunk; 4-inch square of gold solid for star; and 3-inch square of a different bright solid fabric and scrap of gray solid for each lightbulb
All-purpose thread to match fabrics
1/4 yard of paper-backed fusible web
12-inch x 20-inch piece of tear-away stabilizer
White fabric marker or dimensional fabric/craft paint
Standard sewing supplies

Finished Size: The design area measures about 10 inches across x 17-1/2 inches high and is shown on an Adult size Large sweatshirt.

Directions:
Pre-wash all fabrics, washing colors separately. If water is discolored, wash again until rinse water runs clear. Dry and press all fabrics.

Wash and dry sweatshirt according to manufacturer's instructions.

Trace patterns onto folded tracing paper as directed on patterns. Cut out each and unfold for complete patterns.

Trace around the patterns onto paper side of fusible web, leaving 1/2 in. between the shapes and tracing six or any desired number of lightbulbs. Cut the shapes apart, leaving a margin of paper around each.

Fuse shapes onto the wrong side of fabrics as directed on the patterns, with grain lines matching and following manufacturer's directions. Cut shapes out on traced lines.

Remove paper from shapes. Position the star right side up on the center front of sweatshirt about 2 in. from the bottom of the neckline ribbing.

Place the tree trunk, bottom, middle and top tree pieces right side up on the sweatshirt, overlapping the shapes as you add them and making sure the top tree piece is about 1/4 in. below the star. Fuse pieces in place.

Fuse lightbulbs onto tree where desired, overlapping the pieces as shown on pattern.

Pin or baste stabilizer onto wrong side of sweatshirt behind appliques.

Using matching thread and a medium satin stitch, applique around each piece in the same order the shapes were fused to sweatshirt. Remove stabilizer. Pull all loose threads to wrong side and secure.

With fabric craft marker or dimensional fabric paint, write "You light up my life" on the star freehand and add names to the lightbulbs if desired.

With contrasting color of thread and a narrow satin stitch, ruffle-stitch the ribbing on the collar and cuff edges of sweatshirt. To ruffle-stitch, stretch the ribbing both in front of and in back of the needle, keeping the fabric taut as you overcast the edge of the ribbing.

In same way, stitch over the first stitching a second time with a medium satin stitch.

Don this lively apparel for any happy holiday gathering! ★

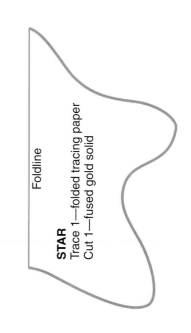

Foldline

STAR
Trace 1—folded tracing paper
Cut 1—fused gold solid

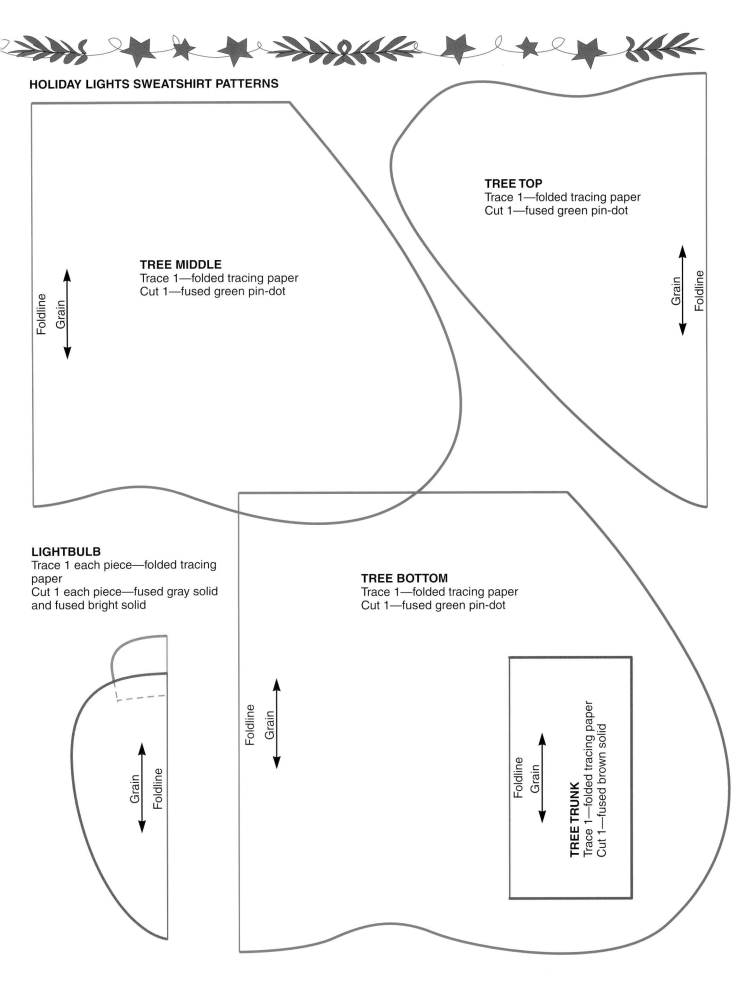

HOLIDAY LIGHTS SWEATSHIRT PATTERNS

TREE MIDDLE
Trace 1—folded tracing paper
Cut 1—fused green pin-dot

Foldline
Grain

TREE TOP
Trace 1—folded tracing paper
Cut 1—fused green pin-dot

Grain
Foldline

LIGHTBULB
Trace 1 each piece—folded tracing
paper
Cut 1 each piece—fused gray solid
and fused bright solid

Grain
Foldline

TREE BOTTOM
Trace 1—folded tracing paper
Cut 1—fused green pin-dot

Foldline
Grain

Foldline
Grain

TREE TRUNK
Trace 1—folded tracing paper
Cut 1—fused brown solid

Gingerbread Recipe Holder Adds Spice to Any Kitchen

YOU'LL WANT to tuck all your keepsake holiday recipes into this gay little gingerbread girl's pocket for safekeeping! Designer Sheryl Radakovich of Portage, Indiana says the wall hanger stitches up in a wink of Santa's eye and is sure to add festive flair to any Christmas kitchen.

GINGERBREAD RECIPE HOLDER PATTERNS

Trace 1 entire shape—folded tracing paper
Cut as directed in instructions—tan felt

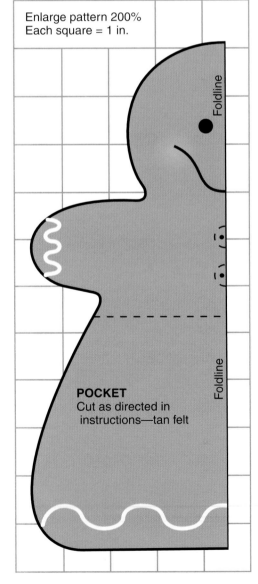

Enlarge pattern 200%
Each square = 1 in.

Foldline

Foldline

POCKET
Cut as directed in instructions—tan felt

Materials Needed:

Pattern below left
Tracing paper and pencil
Three 9-inch x 12-inch pieces of tan felt
Three 8-1/2-inch x 11-1/2-inch pieces of fusible interfacing
Black six-strand embroidery floss
Embroidery needle
1-1/2-inch x 5-inch piece of green-and-white check fabric
Two 5/8-inch dark green two-hole buttons
Dimensional fabric/craft paints—black, red and white
5/8-inch plastic ring for hanger
Powdered cosmetic blush
Cotton swab
Iron and ironing surface
Straight pins
White (tacky) glue
Scissors

Finished Size: Gingerbread recipe holder measures about 8 inches wide x 11 inches high.

Directions:

Use copy machine to enlarge gingerbread pattern to 200% and trace onto folded tracing paper. Or mark tracing paper with a 1-in. grid and draw pattern as shown onto folded tracing paper. Cut out and open for complete pattern.

Center and fuse a piece of interfacing to one side of each felt piece, following manufacturer's instructions.

Place two felt pieces together with edges matching and the fused (interfaced) sides facing. Pin the gingerbread pattern to layered felt pieces. Cut out gingerbread shape.

Cut gingerbread pattern apart along dashed line and discard top piece.

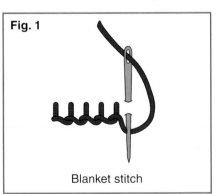

Fig. 1

Blanket stitch

Using pocket pattern, cut one pocket piece from the remaining piece of fused felt.

Using a blanket stitch (see Fig. 1) and unseparated six-strand embroidery floss, stitch along the straight edge of the pocket. Fasten off stitching on back.

Place the pocket, felt side up, on top of the two gingerbread pieces with curved edges matching. Pin as needed to hold. Blanket-stitch around outside edge of gingerbread shape, stitching through all layers.

Hand-sew the plastic ring to the center of back of head with black floss, being careful not to stitch through to front.

Using unseparated black floss, sew the buttons to front of gingerbread where shown on pattern.

Use cotton swab and a circular motion to apply cosmetic blush to cheeks.

With black dimensional paint, make two small dots on the face for the eyes and a long thin curved line for the smile.

With white dimensional paint, add squiggly lines for icing to hands and bottom of dress.

With red dimensional paint, write "Holiday Recipes" freehand on pocket as shown in photo.

Pull a few threads from each edge of green-and-white check fabric strip to create a fringed look. Tie an overhand knot in the center of the fabric strip for bow. Glue bow to top of head where shown in photo.

Tuck a few of your favorite holiday recipes into the pocket of your gingerbread recipe card holder, then hang up in your kitchen. ★

Jolly Door Decor's Inviting

SOMETIMES it's little touches—like this holly jolly door hanger—that do the most to brighten a home for the holidays. Designer Dana Hilts of Fredericksburg, Virginia says, "It can be stitched up in no time...and slipped over any doorknob to extend best wishes to all who enter."

Materials Needed:
Chart below right
7-inch x 9-inch piece of white 14-count Aida cloth
6-1/2-inch x 8-1/2-inch piece of fusible interfacing
6-inch x 8-inch piece of coordinating fabric for backing
DMC six-strand embroidery floss in colors listed on color key
Size 24 tapestry needle
15-inch length of 1/4-inch-wide green satin ribbon for hanger
Polyester fiberfill
Standard sewing supplies

Finished Size: The door hanger is about 5 inches wide x 7 inches high without the hanger. The design area is 87 stitches high x 48 stitches wide.

Directions:
Zigzag or overcast edges of Aida cloth to prevent fraying. Fold Aida cloth in half lengthwise and then in half crosswise to find center and mark this point.

To find center of chart, draw lines across chart connecting arrows. Begin stitching at this point.

Working with 18-in. lengths of six-strand floss, separate strands and use two strands for cross-stitching and French knots and two strands for back-stitching unless otherwise noted on color key. See Fig. 1 for stitch illustrations.

Each square on chart equals one stitch worked over a set of fabric threads. Use colors indicated on color key to complete cross-stitching, then backstitching.

Do not knot floss on back of work. Instead, leave a tail of floss on back of work and hold it in place while working the first few stitches over it. To end a strand, run needle under a few neighboring stitches in back before cutting floss close to work.

ASSEMBLY: Fuse interfacing centered onto wrong side of completed design, following manufacturer's instructions. With stitched design centered, trim Aida cloth to 6 in. x 8 in.

With raw edges even, baste ends of ribbon to top edge of right side of completed design about 1-1/4 in. from side edges for hanger.

Pin the right side of backing fabric to right side of completed design with the raw

edges matching.

Sew pieces together with a 1/2-in. seam allowance, leaving an opening for turning. Trim, leaving a 1/4-in. seam allowance and clip corners diagonally. Turn right side out.

Stuff lightly with polyester fiberfill.

Turn raw edges of opening in and hand-sew opening closed.

Dangle from a doorknob! ★

JOLLY HOLIDAY DOOR HANGER CHART

COLOR KEY	DMC
▣ White	000
＼ Ecru	000
▣ Black	310
◐ Medium Navy Blue	311
▨ Light Navy Blue	312
▣ Holiday Red	321
▼ Dark Holiday Red	498
◉ Bright Holiday Red	666
▪ Medium Pumpkin Spice	721
• Light Beige Gray	822
▼ Ultra Very Light Antique Blue	3753

BACKSTITCHING	
— Medium Navy Blue	311
— Holiday Red	321
— Dark Pewter Gray	413
— Dark Pewter Gray (1 strand)	413
— Light Brown	434
— Holiday Green	699
— Ultra Very Light Antique Blue	3753

FRENCH KNOT

◉ Black	310
◉ Holiday Green	699

Fig. 1

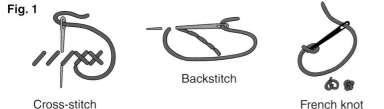

Cross-stitch   Backstitch   French knot

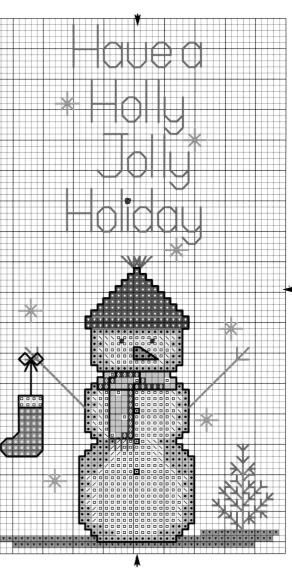

Protect Fa-la-la Finery with Festive Apron

THIS CHRISTMAS APRON is pretty enough to be part of any holiday celebration. "You won't have to change clothes every time you're in the kitchen cooking if you're wearing this apron," assures designer Jean Devore from Jackson, Missouri.

Jean made a matching hot pad from the same bright holiday fabrics—then lined it with protective batting to give busy cooks a handle on the holidays.

Materials Needed (for both):
44-inch-wide 100% cotton fabrics—
1 yard of red solid for piecing, binding and ties, 1/3 yard of green Christmas print for piecing, and 1-1/2 yards of white-on-white print for piecing and backing of apron and hot pad

Red and white all-purpose thread
29-inch square of light-weight quilt batting for apron
10-inch square of Teflon batting or cotton batting for hot pad
Quilter's marking pen or pencil
Quilter's ruler
Rotary cutter and mat (optional)
Standard sewing supplies

Finished Size: Apron measures about 27-1/4 inches across x 27-1/4 inches long without ties. Hot pad measures about 9-1/2 inches square.

Directions:
Pre-wash fabrics, washing each color separately. If water is discolored, wash again until the rinse water runs clear. Dry and press all fabrics.

CUTTING: Cut fabrics using rotary cutter and quilter's ruler, or mark fabrics using ruler and marker of choice and cut with scissors. Cut strips crosswise from selvage to selvage.

From green Christmas print, cut five 1-1/2-in.-wide strips for piecing nine-patch squares.

From red solid, cut four 1-1/2-in.-wide strips for piecing nine-patch squares and seven 2-1/2-in.-wide strips for binding and ties.

From white-on-white print, cut one 29-in. square for backing of apron. Also cut six 9-1/2-in. squares and twenty 3-1/2-in. squares for apron blocks and for hot pad.

PIECING: Do all piecing with accurate 1/4-in. seams, matching thread, right sides of fabrics together and raw edges matching. Press seams toward darker fabrics unless otherwise directed.

Small nine-patch block: Sew a 1-1/2-in.-wide green Christmas print strip to both long edges of two 1-1/2-in.-wide solid red strips to make two green, red, green 3-1/2-in.-wide pieced strips. From these pieced strips, cut fifty 1-1/2-in.-wide sections as shown in Fig. 1.

In the same way, sew a 1-1/2-in.-wide red solid strip to both long edges of a 1-1/2-in.-wide green Christmas print strip to make a red, green, red 3-1/2-in.-wide pieced strip. From this pieced strip, cut twenty-five 1-1/2-in.-wide sections as before.

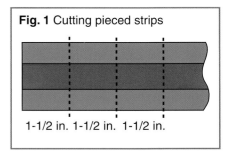

Fig. 1 Cutting pieced strips

1-1/2 in.   1-1/2 in.   1-1/2 in.

Sew two green, red, green pieced sections to a red, green, red pieced section as shown in Fig. 2 to make a 3-1/2-in. square small nine-patch block.

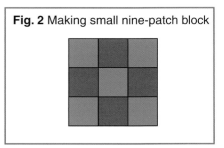

Fig. 2 Making small nine-patch block

In the same way, sew the remaining pieced sections together, making a total of 25 small nine-patch blocks.

Large nine-patch block: Lay out five small nine-patch squares and four 3-1/2-in. white-on-white print squares in three rows with three squares in each row as shown in Fig. 3.

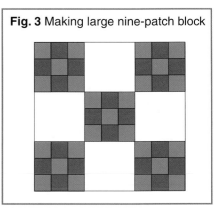

Fig. 3 Making large nine-patch block

Sew squares in each row together as planned. Then sew the rows together,

carefully matching corners to make a 9-1/2-in. square large nine-patch block. Repeat to make a total of five large nine-patch blocks.

APRON: Lay out four 9-1/2-in. large nine-patch blocks and five 9-1/2-in. white-on-white print squares in three rows with three blocks in each row, alternating the blocks to make a checkerboard pattern. Set remaining large nine-patch square and 9-1/2-in. white-on-white print square aside for hot pad.

Sew blocks in each row together and then sew the rows together as planned, carefully matching corners.

Using quilter's marking pen or pencil, mark quilting lines on each white square by extending the seam lines of the pieced nine-patch squares through each white square.

Place white-on-white print backing fabric wrong side up on a flat surface. Place batting centered over backing. Center pieced apron front right side up on top of batting. Smooth out wrinkles.

Hand-baste all layers together, stitching from center to corners, then horizontally and vertically every 4 in.

With white thread, machine-quilt along marked lines and around the outside edges of each small nine-patch square.

With quilter's marking pen, mark the cutting lines for the apron as shown in Fig. 4. Cut out through all layers on marked lines.

Sew through all layers, stitching 1/8 in. from outside edges of apron. Remove basting and marking lines.

Binding and ties: Cut two 20-in.-long pieces from a red solid binding strip for waist ties. Press the long edges and one short edge of each 1/8 in. to wrong side twice. With red thread, sew close to first fold of each to hem.

Baste raw edges of ties to opposite sides of waist on back of apron with raw edges even and hemmed top edge of tie 1/2 in. from waist edge.

Cut a 12-in.-long piece from another red solid binding strip for binding the top (bib) of apron. Press strip in half lengthwise with wrong sides together.

Sew binding strip to right side of top of apron with raw edges matching and a 1/4-in. seam. Fold binding to back, encasing raw edges. Using red thread, hand- or machine-sew fold of binding to back of apron.

Sew the short edges of two remaining binding strips together to make one long strip. Press strip in half lengthwise with wrong sides together.

Starting at one waist edge and with ends of ties pinned to the back, sew binding to front of apron as before, mi-

tering each bottom corner. Trim excess. Fold binding to back, encasing raw edges and sew fold of binding to back of apron as before.

Fold one short edge of two remaining binding strips 1/4 in. to wrong side. Press each strip in half lengthwise with wrong sides together.

Pin a binding strip to front of apron with folded end even with edge of previous binding at waist edge. Sew binding to curved edge as before. Fold binding to back, encasing raw edges and pin.

For neck tie, sew long edges of free end of binding strip together with a straight stitch. Stitch binding around curved edge of apron as before. Repeat for other tie and binding of remaining curved edge of apron.

HOT PAD: Place 9-1/2-in. square of white-on-white print fabric wrong side up on a flat surface. Center square of Teflon batting or cotton batting on top of backing. Place remaining large nine-patch square right side up over batting. Smooth out wrinkles.

Hand-baste all layers together as needed to hold.

With white thread, machine-quilt along outer edges of small nine-patch blocks.

Sew around outside edge of pieced

square, stitching 1/8 in. from edge. Trim batting and backing even with edges of pieced square. Remove basting.

Binding and hanging loop: Fold short edge of remaining binding strip 1/4 in. to wrong side. Press strip in half lengthwise with wrong sides together.

Starting at one corner, sew binding to right side of hot pad with raw edges matching and a 1/4-in. seam, mitering corners. Extend binding 3 in. beyond beginning corner for hanging loop.

Fold binding to back, encasing raw edges. Using matching thread, hand- or machine-sew fold of binding to back of hot pad. Sew long edges of hanging loop together. To form hanging loop, sew short end of binding to back of hot pad.

Model your pretty patchwork apron this holiday season! ★

Hostess Tip

● To allow more time to mingle with guests, plan a menu with make-ahead dishes that can easily be reheated in the oven or microwave.

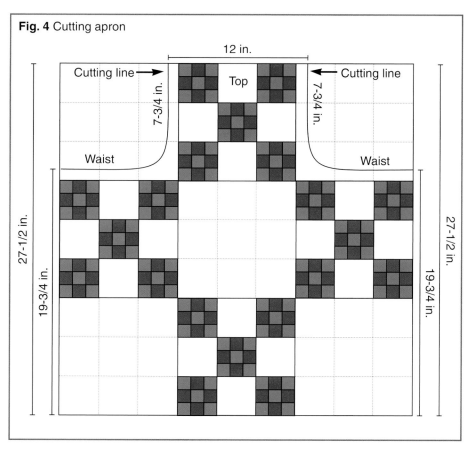

Fig. 4 Cutting apron

Cutting line → Top ← Cutting line
12 in.
7-3/4 in.
7-3/4 in.
Waist Waist
27-1/2 in.
27-1/2 in.
19-3/4 in.
19-3/4 in.

Puzzle Celebrates the Reason for the Season

KIDS can easily piece together the true meaning of Christmas, thanks to this three-piece Nativity puzzle. Crafter Mary Nelson of Dresden, New York used wood and bright acrylic paints to create the fanciful puzzle of the infant, a watchful guardian angel and the message "Oh, holy night."

Materials Needed:

Pattern on next page
Tracing paper and pencil
8-inch x 10-inch length of 1-1/4-inch-thick pine (1-1/4-inch pine is actually 1 inch thick)
Scroll or band saw
Sandpaper and tack cloth
Water container
Foam plate or palette
Paper towels
Acrylic craft paints (Mary used Deco Art Americana paints)—
Antique Mauve, Burnt Umber, Buttermilk, Flesh Tone, Honey Brown, Lamp Black, Leaf Green, Light Cinnamon, Marigold, Midnite Blue, Moon Yellow, Petal Pink, Sable Brown, True Ochre, White Wash and Wisteria
Paintbrushes—3/4-inch wash, 1/2-inch shader, No. 2 shader and liner
Toothbrush or spatter brush
Toothpick
Cotton swab
Newspapers
Acrylic spray sealer

3/4-inch x 12-inch torn strip of tan and blue plaid fabric for bow
Glue gun and glue stick
Scissors

Finished Size: Puzzle measures about 9-1/4 inches tall x 6-1/2 inches wide x 1 inch thick.

Directions:

Trace pattern on next page onto tracing paper. Turn traced pattern over and rub back of design with a soft lead pencil. Turn pattern right side up and center it on pine wood piece. Retrace the cutting lines with a dull pencil, transferring design onto wood.

Cut out along outline and inside cutting lines of wood shapes with band or scroll saw. Sand to smooth so pieces fit together easily. Wipe with tack cloth to remove sanding dust.

PAINTING: Place small amounts of paint on foam plate or palette as needed. Paint as directed, extending paints to edges and back of each piece. Apply additional coats of paint as needed for complete coverage. Let paint dry between each application.

Refer to pattern and photo while painting as directed in instructions that follow.

Sky: Use 3/4-inch wash brush and Midnite Blue to paint the sky.

Use 1/2-in. shader and Marigold to paint star.

Thin White Wash with clean water to an ink-like consistency. Use 1/2-inch shader to apply mixture around outside edge of the sky to highlight. Using same thinned paint and liner, write "Oh, holy night" on sky under star.

Dip toothpick into White Wash and use to dab dots on letters as shown on pattern.

For random small stars, use liner and Marigold to paint a tiny X. Then dip toothpick into Marigold and use to dab a tiny dot in the center of each X.

Angel and baby: Use No. 2 shader and Flesh Tone to paint the face and hands of the angel and baby.

Use No. 2 shader and Sable Brown to shade the face and hands of each.

To shade, dip paintbrush into clean water. Touch the brush onto a paper towel so the brush is wet but not dripping wet. Touch corner of brush into paint, then stroke the brush on a clean area of the foam plate or palette to blend the paint and water. The color should fade from dark to light to clear. Pull the paint-filled edge of the brush along the edge to be shaded.

Using a nearly dry cotton swab and a circular motion, apply Antique Mauve to the cheeks of both the angel and the baby.

Dip toothpick in Lamp Black and use to dab two tiny dots for the baby's eyes.

Use liner and Lamp Black to paint angel's eyes, eyelashes, the baby's hair and the mouths and eyebrows of both.

Use No. 2 shader and Light Cinnamon to paint angel's hair. When dry, shade outer edges with Burnt Umber.

Use 1/2-in. shader and Buttermilk to paint angel's wings.

Use No. 2 shader and Burnt Umber to shade wings.

Use liner and Burnt Umber to add lines to hair.

Use 1/2-in. shader and Wisteria to paint angel's dress. When dry, shade with Midnite Blue to define sleeves of dress and to outline the baby and cradle.

Use end of smallest paintbrush handle and Buttermilk and White Wash to add alternating colors of dots to form collar and cuffs on angel's dress.

Using liner and Leaf Green, paint leaves of flowers on dress.

Dip end of smallest paintbrush handle in Petal Pink and use to dab a small dot for petal of each flower. In same way, add two Antique Mauve dots for remaining petals of flowers.

Cradle: Use 3/4-in. wash brush and Sable Brown to paint cradle.

Use No. 2 shader and Burnt Umber to shade, creating boards on the cradle.

Dip toothpick in Lamp Black and use to dab on tiny dots for nails on cradle.

Use liner and Honey Brown, True Ochre, Burnt Umber and Moon Yellow in that order to paint straw along top edge of cradle.

FINISHING: Protect work surface with newspapers. Thin White Wash with clean water to an ink-like consistency. Brush thinned paint onto toothbrush or spatter brush.

If using a spatter brush, follow brush manufacturer's directions to spatter the paint onto all the puzzle pieces. If using toothbrush, hold bristles of toothbrush about 6 inches from surface and pull your thumbnail or a paintbrush handle toward you over the bristles to spatter paint.

Repeat to spatter Sable Brown onto angel and baby only.

Spray all sides of each piece with acrylic sealer following manufacturer's

instructions. Allow to dry thoroughly. If the grain of the wood rises where the pieces fit together, lightly sand the raised grain. Spray again with sealer.

Gently pull a couple of threads out of each side of fabric strip to fringe the edges. Then tie the fabric strip into a small bow. Glue bow to angel. Trim the ends of the bow to desired length.

Grace your home with this meaningful holiday accent. ★

WOODEN NATIVITY PATTERN
Trace 1—tracing paper
Cut 1 each puzzle piece—1-1/4-in. pine
Paint as directed in instructions

Oh, holy night

Cutting line

Cutting line

Cutting line

Grain

Snowman Keeps Candy Canes at Arm's Length

GOT AN HOUR? That's just about how long it takes to follow Sandy Rollinger's directions for crafting this jolly snowman candy-cane holder.

"I like fast-and-easy projects," explains the Apollo, Pennsylvania artisan, who muffled her frosty fellow in Christmas colors. Stand him in your front hall to greet friends and carolers with welcoming armfuls of treats.

Materials Needed:
Patterns on this page and next page
Tracing paper and pencil
Scissors
Graphite paper
Stylus or dry ballpoint pen

10-inch length of 1 x 6 pine for snowman and mittens (1-inch pine is actually 3/4 inch thick)
6-inch length of 2 x 6 pine for base (2-inch pine is actually 1-1/2 inches thick)
Scroll or band saw
5/16-inch wooden dowels—two 4-1/4-inch lengths and two 1-inch lengths
Drill with 5/16-inch bit
Sandpaper and tack cloth
Paper towels
Water container
Foam plate or palette
Acrylic craft paints—black, blue, green, orange, red and white
Dimensional paints—black, green and red
Paintbrushes—5/8-inch flat, 1/2-inch angular shader, 1/4-inch flat, small round and liner
4-1/2-inch x 6-inch piece of white felt for covering bottom of base
1/2-inch green pom-pom
Wood glue
Powdered cosmetic blush
Cotton swab
Textured snow medium
Candy canes

Finished Size: Snowman is about 10-1/2 inches high x 14 inches across.

Directions:
Trace patterns onto tracing paper and cut out. With grain lines matching, trace around snowman and mitten patterns onto 1 x 6 pine as directed on patterns. Trace around base pattern onto 2 x 6 pine. Cut out wood pieces using a scroll or band saw.

Using 5/16-inch bit, drill a 1/2-in.-deep hole into each mitten where shown on pattern. Drill two 1/2-in.-deep holes into wood base and two matching holes into bottom of snowman. Drill a hole into each side of snowman at neck area for arm dowels.

Sand all wooden pieces to smooth. Wipe each with tack cloth to remove sanding dust.

Place small amounts of paint on foam plate or palette as needed. Paint as directed, extending paint around edges and back of each wooden piece. Paint boots, mittens, hat and snowman body the same on

SNOWMAN BASE PATTERN
Trace 1—tracing paper
Cut 1—2 x 6 pine
Cut 1—white felt

←—Drill holes—→

←— Grain —→

both sides. Extend scarf around neck on back of snowman. Apply additional coats of paint as needed for complete coverage. Let dry between each application.

Refer to pattern and photo while painting as directed below.

Use 5/8-in. flat brush to paint all wooden pieces white. When dry, sand each piece lightly. Wipe with tack cloth to remove sanding dust.

Place snowman pattern on top of snowman with edges matching. Slip graphite paper between pattern and wood. Trace over inside design lines with stylus or dry ballpoint pen to transfer hat, face, scarf and boots onto one side of the snowman cutout. In the same way, transfer the hat and boots onto the back of the cutout.

Dip the 1/2-in. angular shader into clean water. Touch the brush to a paper towel until brush is wet but not dripping. Touch longer corner of the brush into blue paint, then stroke the brush on a clean area of the palette or foam plate to blend the paint and water. The color should fade from dark to light to clear.

Pulling the paint-filled edge of the brush along the edge to be shaded, shade the outside edges of snowman. Also shade above the boot area, around the scarf and under the hat. Shade the back and the sides of these areas in the same way.

Lightly brush blue all over entire snowman to create an icy look.

Using 5/8-in. flat brush, paint boot areas black, mittens red and the hat and scarf green.

To highlight scarf, dip the 5/8-in. flat brush into green paint. Then dip one corner of the brush into white. With one brush stroke, paint horizontally across scarf with the green along the bottom edge of scarf. Repeat process for sides and back of scarf. Load the brush in the same way and paint the scarf ends with a single vertical stroke. With the same brush, highlight across the top of the scarf knot with white.

Use a round brush to add green fringe to the ends of the scarf.

Add strokes of green and white to hat following the vertical contour of the hat and brim, using 1/4-in. flat brush. Blend strokes slightly.

Use red dimensional paint to add curved lines to hat brim and dots to rest of hat and to scarf.

Add dots of green dimensional paint to mittens.

Use cotton swab and a circular motion to apply cosmetic blush to cheeks.

Use round brush to paint nose orange.

Use liner to add tiny white lines to top of nose for highlights.

Add two black dimensional paint dots for eyes and six dots for mouth.

Apply glue to the two 1-in. dowels. Insert one end of each dowel into drilled holes on bottom of boot area and other end into matching holes of base. Press pieces together so snowman stands flush on base.

Apply glue onto one end of each arm dowel and insert that end into a mitten. Glue other end of each arm dowel in-

to neck area, making sure mitten thumbs are pointed up.

Cut out and glue felt to bottom of base. Glue green pom-pom to top of hat.

Use 5/8-in. flat brush to apply a thick layer of textured snow to top and sides of base. Use brush to make swirls in snow. In same way, add textured snow to top of dowel arms. Let dry.

Hang candy canes on the arms. ★

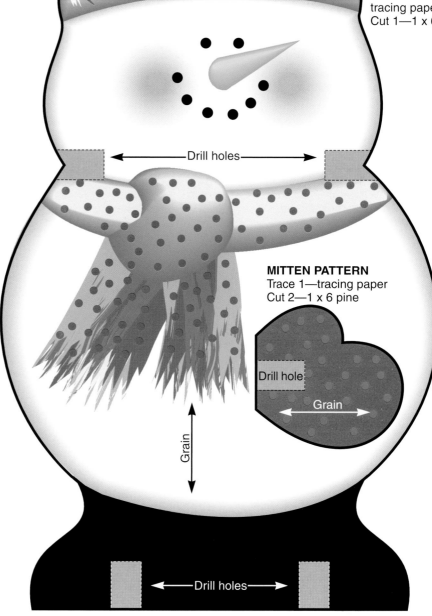

SNOWMAN PATTERN
Trace 1—tracing paper
Cut 1—1 x 6 pine

Drill holes

MITTEN PATTERN
Trace 1—tracing paper
Cut 2—1 x 6 pine

Drill hole

Grain

Grain

Drill holes

101

Sparkly Snowflakes Put Punch in Holidays!

YOU'LL FEEL just like one of Santa's elves tapping out the tin-punch designs on these dazzling snowflakes!

Sandra Graham Smith dreamed up this idea to brighten her own Florissant, Missouri home, and she's already made a blizzard of snowflakes to hang on her tree.

"I also use tiny suction cups to hang them in my windows," Sandra says. "Light shines through the holes by day, and at night they catch and reflect all the holiday lights."

Materials Needed (for both):
Patterns on next page
Tracing paper
Scissors
Black permanent marker
8-inch x 12-inch sheet of aluminum flashing (found in hardware stores)
Tin snips
Masking tape
1-1/2-inch finishing nails
Hammer
Pressed wood board or other hard protective surface
Red acrylic faceted cabochons—one 25mm round, four 10mm round and four 8mm x 18mm navettes (teardrop shapes) for red snowflake
Green glitter dimensional fabric/craft paint for green snowflake
10-inch length each of 1/8-inch-wide red and green satin ribbon for hangers
E-6000 glue or jewelry glue

Finished Size: Red snowflake measures about 6 inches across and green snowflake measures about 5-3/8 inches across without hangers.

Directions:
Trace patterns including all dot positions onto tracing paper with marker. Cut out pattern with scissors. Trace around the pattern onto aluminum flashing with a marker.

Use tin snips to cut out each snowflake design, cutting just inside traced lines.

Place pattern on matching snowflake with edges matching. Use masking tape to secure pattern.

Place a snowflake on hard surface. Punch dots on design using hammer and nail. Hold snowflake up to light to

make sure nail has pierced the surface. Punch a larger hole at the top of each snowflake for hanger. Remove pattern and tape. Smooth side is the back of the snowflake.

Referring to photo above for placement, glue red jewels inside punched shapes on red snowflake design. Let dry.

Referring to photo for placement, apply green glitter paint inside punched shapes on green snowflake design. Let dry.

Thread end of red ribbon through hole for hanger on the red jeweled snowflake and end of green ribbon through hole for hanger on green jeweled snowflake.

Knot each ribbon 2 in. from snowflake and tie ends of each in a bow. Trim ribbon ends as desired. ★

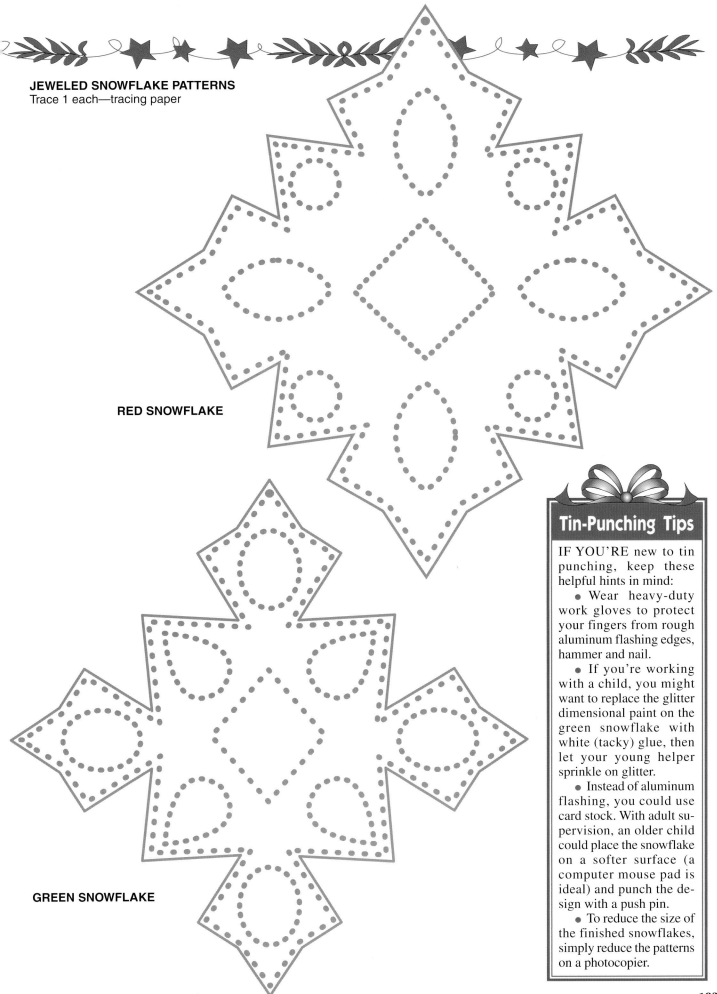

JEWELED SNOWFLAKE PATTERNS
Trace 1 each—tracing paper

RED SNOWFLAKE

GREEN SNOWFLAKE

Tin-Punching Tips

IF YOU'RE new to tin punching, keep these helpful hints in mind:

• Wear heavy-duty work gloves to protect your fingers from rough aluminum flashing edges, hammer and nail.

• If you're working with a child, you might want to replace the glitter dimensional paint on the green snowflake with white (tacky) glue, then let your young helper sprinkle on glitter.

• Instead of aluminum flashing, you could use card stock. With adult supervision, an older child could place the snowflake on a softer surface (a computer mouse pad is ideal) and punch the design with a push pin.

• To reduce the size of the finished snowflakes, simply reduce the patterns on a photocopier.

Rudolph Makes an 'Endeering' Favor

TUCK these whimsical reindeer into candy cups and rein in a sleighful of compliments from holiday dinner guests! Or use them as plant pokes to perk up a Christmas cactus.

Patricia Klesh of Martinsville, New Jersey includes directions so easy to follow that you'll want to dash away now and start crafting a herd.

Materials Needed:
One jumbo craft stick
1/16-inch-thick purchased wooden cutouts—one 1-3/4-inch-long teardrop for head and two 1-1/2-inch-long teardrops for ears (Patricia used Woodsies shapes)
Brown acrylic craft paint
Small flat paintbrush
5-inch length of 6mm dark brown pipe cleaner (chenille stem)
One 1/4-inch red pom-pom
Two 10mm glue-on wiggle eyes

One 1-3/4-inch mini artificial green wreath
5-inch length of plastic mini lightbulb garland
Glue gun and glue sticks

Finished Size: Party favor is about 3 inches across x 7-3/4 inches long.

Directions:
Glue the two 1-1/2-inch-long teardrop shapes to rounded end of 1-3/4-inch-long teardrop shape with points outward and upward to form ears on head.

Glue head to one end of jumbo craft stick with head overlapped 1 in.

Paint entire piece brown. Let dry.

Glue pom-pom to pointed end of head for nose.

Glue wiggle eyes to head below ears.

Slide wreath up craft stick below nose and glue to craft stick as needed to secure in place.

Fold pipe cleaner in half. Glue fold be-

tween ears on back of head for antlers. Shape antlers as shown in photo.

Glue one end of mini lightbulb garland behind tip of one ear. Wrap garland around antlers. Glue other end of garland behind tip of other ear. Spot-glue garland to antlers to hold.

Place your Rudolph in a plastic cup or dish filled with Christmas candy and perch on your holiday table! ★

Yule Earmark This Fun Look!

LOOKING FOR unique stocking stuffers or a gift for a favorite teacher? These holiday earrings from crafter Connie Folse of Thibodaux, Louisiana will have you smiling from ear to ear!

The frosty fellows are really tiny erasers decked out in Christmas colors. "They work up in just minutes using scraps of crochet thread," says Connie, who rates this project "beginner-easy".

Materials Needed:
Size 10 crochet cotton—small amount each of red and green

Size 5 steel crochet hook
Two earring wires
Two 7/8-inch-tall snowman erasers or snowman novelty buttons
White (tacky) glue
Tapestry or yarn needle
Scissors

Finished Size: Each earring measures about 1-1/2 inches across.

Directions:
Round 1: With red, ch 2, work 6 scs in second ch from hk, join with a sl st in first sc: 6 scs.

Round 2: Ch 1, work 2 scs in same st, work 2 scs in each of the next scs around, join with a sl st in first sc: 12 scs.

Round 3: Ch 1, sc in same st, * work 2 scs in next sc, sc in next sc; repeat from * around to last sc, work 2 scs in last sc, join with a sl st in first sc: 18 scs.

Round 4: Repeat Round 2: 36 scs.

Round 5: Ch 1, sc in same st, ch 3, sk next st, work 1 sc in next st, [work 1 sc in next st, ch 3, sk next st, work 1 sc in next st] 11 times, join with a sl st to first sc. Fasten off: 12 ch-3 sps.

Round 6: With right side facing and

a green sl knot on hk, sc in any sk sc of Round 5, * ch 3, sc in back of next sk sc, ch 3, sc in front of next sk sc; repeat from * around to last sk sc, ch 3, sc in back of last sk sc, ch 3, join with a sl st to first sc. Fasten off.

Use tapestry or yarn needle to weave in all loose ends.

Attach an earring wire to each crocheted piece in any red ch-3 sp of Round 5.

Glue a snowman eraser or snowman button to the right side of each crocheted piece as shown in photo below left. Let dry.

Model at your next holiday gathering!

ABBREVIATIONS

ch(s)	chain(s)
hk	hook
sc(s)	single crochet(s)
sk	skip
sl knot	slip knot
sl st	slip stitch
st	stitch
sp(s)	space(s)
* or [ ]	Instructions following asterisk or within brackets are repeated as instructed.

Knit Skirt Circles the Tree

BUTTON UP your balsam in cable stitches and country style with this cozy knit tree skirt designed by Marion Cornett of Fowlerville, Michigan.

Marion recommends this project for experienced knitters who happen to know a few basic crochet stitches, too.

Materials Needed:
28 ounces of red 4-ply worsted-weight yarn (Marion used Caron Sayelle yarn No. 326 Scarlet)
Size 5 (3.75mm) 47- or 60-inch-long circular knitting needle or size needed to obtain correct gauge
Cable needle
Six stitch markers
Six stitch holders
Size G/6 (4.25mm) crochet hook
Tapestry or yarn needle
Scissors

Finished Size: Tree skirt measures about 48 inches across.

Gauge: Working in St st, 5 sts and 7 rows = 1 inch.

Stitches Used:
STOCKINETTE STITCH: St st:
Row 1 (RS): K across row.
Row 2 (WS): P across row.
Repeat Rows 1 and 2 as directed.
C2F: Place next 2 sts on cable needle and hold at front, k 2, k 2 from cable needle.
C2B: Place next 2 sts on cable needle and hold at back, k 2, k 2 from cable needle.

Directions:
This piece is worked back and forth in rows on a circular needle. Do not work in rounds.
Cast on 105 sts.
TOP Row 1 (RS): * K 15, place stitch marker; repeat from * across row to last 15 sts, k 15: 105 sts, (15 sts at each end and between stitch markers).
Row 2: * K 1, p 6, k 1, p 6, k 1; repeat from * across row: 105 sts.
Row 3: * K 7, pick up horizontal lp of row below (between sts) and k this st, k in front and back of next st, k 7; repeat from * across row: 119 sts, (17 sts at each end and between stitch markers).
Row 4 and all even-numbered rows (WS): At each end and between stitch markers [K 1, p 6, k 1, p to last 8 sts, k 1, p 6, k 1].
Row 5: At each end and between stitch markers [K 1, C2F, k 2, k in front

and back of next st, k to last 8 sts, k 1 in front and back of next st, C2F, k 3].
Row 7: At each end and between stitch markers [K 7, k in front and back of next st, k to last 8 sts, k in front and back of next st, k 7].
Row 9: At each end and between stitch markers [K 3, C2B, k in front and back of next st, k to last 8 sts, k in front and back of next st, k 2, C2B, k 1].
Row 11: Repeat Row 7.
Repeat Rows 5-12 until there are 63 sts at each end and between all stitch markers.
Work Rows 5 and 6 once more: 65 sts at each end and between stitch markers.
SEPARATION Row 1 (RS): The sections at each end and between stitch markers will now be worked separately. Keeping to established cable pattern, work first 7 sts, k in front and back of next st, k to last 8 sts, k in front and back of next st, keeping to established cable pattern, work last 7 sts to marker: 67 sts.
 * Place next 65 sts on stitch holder; repeat from * until six stitch holders have been used.
Row 2 and all even-numbered rows (WS): K 1, p 6, k 1, p 51, k 1, p 6, k 1: 67 sts.
Row 3: Keeping to established cable pattern, work first 7 sts, p 1, k 51, p 1, keeping to established cable pattern, work last 7 sts: 67 sts.
Repeat Rows 2 and 3 until section measures 10 in. from Separation Row 1, ending with a RS row.
BORDER Row 1 (WS): K 1, p 6, k across to last 7 sts, p 6, k 1: 67 sts.
Row 2: Keeping to established cable pattern, work first 7 sts, p 1, k 51, p 1, keeping to established cable pattern, work last 7 sts: 67 sts.
Rows 3-9: Repeat Rows 1 and 2: 67 sts.
Bind off.
Transfer sts from next stitch holder onto needle, attach yarn and work as for first section.
Repeat with each remaining section.
TOP RIBBING: With RS facing, pick up cast-on sts along top edge.
Work in k 1, p 1 ribbing for 1-1/2 in., ending with a WS row.
Bind off in k 1, p 1 ribbing, but do not break yarn.
EDGING: Insert crochet hk into last lp on needle, sc in same st. Referring to Figs. 1a-c above right, work 1 reverse sc

in each st around entire piece to 10 in. from top edge on opposite side. Do not fasten off.
BUTTONHOLES: Ch 5 for first buttonhole, sk 1/2 in., continue working in reverse sc to 5 in. from top, ch 5, sk 1/2 in. for next buttonhole, continue working in reverse sc to 1/2 in. from top, ch 5, sk 1/2 in. for top buttonhole. Fasten off on top corner for buttonhole.
Use tapestry or yarn needle to weave in all loose ends.
BUTTONS: With RS facing and with slip knot on crochet hk, insert hk in center of opposite edge corresponding to top buttonhole, ch 5, work 1 sc in second ch from hk and in each remaining ch, join with a sl st in last ch made of beginning ch-5. Fasten off. Use tapestry or yarn needle and tails of yarn to fasten button to tree skirt and to weave in all loose ends.
Repeat for remaining two buttons.

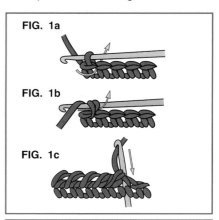

FIG. 1a

FIG. 1b

FIG. 1c

ABBREVIATIONS

ch(s)	chain(s)
hk	hook
k	knit
lp	loop
p	purl
RS	right side
sc(s)	single crochet(s)
sk	skip
sl	slip
st(s)	stitch(es)
WS	wrong side
* or [ ]	Instructions following asterisk or within brackets are repeated as instructed.

Holiday Basket Is Handy Way to Present Gifts

CHOCK-FULL of holiday cheer, this hefty handled container is easy to carry and sports a festive trim of fat sassy snowmen. It looks oh-so-Christmasy sitting in the center of a table or tucked under a tree.

Crafter Mary Cosgrove of Rockville, Connecticut packs her plastic canvas baskets full of cookies, candies or casseroles for family and friends. "It's two gifts in one," she beams.

Materials Needed:

Charts on next page
7-count plastic canvas—one 10-1/2-inch x 13-1/2-inch sheet of white, one 10-1/2-inch x 13-1/2-inch sheet of clear and one 9-inch round plastic canvas shape for bottom
4-ply worsted-weight yarn or plastic canvas yarn—64 yards of white, 19 yards of red and 18 yards of green (Mary used Needloft plastic canvas yarn—#41 White, #02 Red and #28 Green)
1-1/2 yards of black braid (Mary used Kreinik Heavy Braid #32005HL)
Size 18 plastic canvas needle or tapestry needle
Compass
Pencil
9-inch square of white felt
White (tacky) glue
Scissors

Finished Size: Snowman basket measures about 8-1/4 inches across x 5-1/2 inches high, including handles.

Directions:

CUTTING: Remembering to count the bars and not the holes, cut plastic canvas pieces as directed below.

From clear plastic canvas, cut two 20-bar x 91-bar pieces for sides of basket and two 4-bar x 44-bar pieces for the handles.

From white plastic canvas, cut two 20-bar x 91-bar pieces for lining the basket.

Cut off four bars from the outside edge of the round plastic canvas shape, leaving a total of 54 bars across.

STITCHING: Working with 18-in. to 20-in. lengths of yarn or braid, follow charts and instructions to stitch pieces.

Do not knot strand on back of work. Instead, leave a 1-in. tail of yarn on the back of the plastic canvas and work the next few stitches over it. To end, run strand of yarn on back of canvas under completed stitches of the same color and clip close to work.

To make basket sides, overlap six bars on one short end of the two 20-bar x 91-bar clear plastic canvas pieces. Following charts and referring to Fig. 1 for stitch illustrations, fill in the side of basket as shown, stitching a total of 10 snowmen, five worked in red with a

green background and five worked in green with a red background. Overlap short ends and stitch last row of Symrna Cross stitches through both layers.

Using black braid, add French knots for the eyes.

Backstitch mouths with black braid.

Backstitch over one bar with red for each nose.

Using white, add a French knot to top of each snowman's hat.

To make lining of basket, overlap short ends of the two 20-bar x 91-bar pieces of white canvas pieces to fit inside sides of basket. Whipstitch overlapped ends together with white. Slip lining inside the sides of the basket.

Fill in center of each handle with white Symrna Cross stitches. Overcast long edges of each handle with white.

Position handles opposite each other, aligning ends of handles with Symrna Cross stitches on basket sides at top edge. Using white, whipstitch top edges of sides of basket and lining together, catching handles in stitching.

If desired, fill in bottom of round plastic canvas shape with white Continental stitches. Stitch in circles over two bars, starting on the third hole from the outside edge. Occasionally, two stitches will need to be worked in one hole to keep stitches at an angle.

Using white, whipstitch outside edges of bottom piece to bottom edges of sides of basket and lining.

Use compass and pencil to draw an 8-in. circle on white felt. Cut out felt circle. Glue felt circle to inside of bottom of basket.

Fill with Christmas goodies. ★

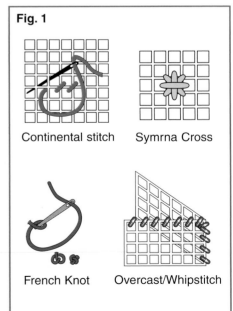

Fig. 1

Continental stitch   Symrna Cross

French Knot   Overcast/Whipstitch

PLASTIC CANVAS BASKET CHARTS

SIDES
20 bars x 91 bars
Cut 2—clear plastic canvas

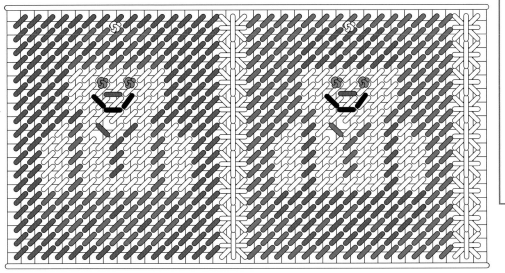

COLOR AND STITCH KEY
CONTINENTAL STITCH
🖊 Green
🖊 Red
🖊 White
SMYRNA CROSS
✳ White
FRENCH KNOT
🌀 Black
🌀 White
BACKSTITCH
— Red
— Black
OVERCAST/WHIPSTITCH
▭ White

HANDLE
4 bars x 44 bars
Cut 2—clear plastic canvas

Rustic Trims Capture a Slice of Christmas

ANY WAY you slice it, Christmas is an inspiration—and for country women, making merry may mean making do with what's at hand. What's at hand for Linda Christie is a whole forest of inspiration for crafting Yuletide trims.

Trees cover more than half the 100-acre farm Linda and her husband, Ken, have lived on for nearly four decades in Acworth, New Hampshire. "I've always enjoyed painting, even as a little girl, and we're kind of a crafty family…so we came up with the idea of painting our own wooden ornaments for Christmas," she recalls.

That was 20 years ago, back when the couple was raising a son and a daughter—and white-faced Herefords.

"Today, we're down to two cats," Linda says with a laugh. But they're still turning out their cheery ornaments.

Ken cuts the wood slices from live cherry, ash and oak trees on their farm. "The branches have to be just the right size—nothing over 3 inches in diameter," Linda explains.

"Once each slice is thoroughly dried

CUT AND DRIED. Linda Christie (above left) says cardinal ornaments (above) are popular—she paints two for every other kind!

(about 2 weeks), he sands it and gives it to me to paint."

Using acrylic paints and tiny brushes, Linda covers the slices with whimsical holiday figures or realistic birds and animals. She coats them with plastic sealer to keep them from chipping, signs each one and then tops it with a bright ribbon.

Not long ago, the couple branched out into making picture frames, magnets and basswood wall clocks to sell along with their ornaments at holiday craft fairs and on the Internet.

"We've learned a lot through trial and error over the years," Linda says. "Like…you can't dry birch without the bark coming off!"

But with a holiday business that is still growing, Linda clearly isn't barking up the wrong tree with her rustic Yuletide trims.

Editor's Note: *To order Linda's ornaments, frames or wall clocks, visit www.christiescountrycrafts.com or call 1-603/835-6521.* ★

A Child's Gift

On the day after Christmas, 'bout quarter past eight,
The rest of the family was sleeping in late…
But I, with my coffee, had slumped in a chair,
And felt the oncoming of post-Christmas despair.

It had all come so quickly, and now, it was done—
The shopping, the feasting, the gifts and the fun.
The presents I'd bought with exceeding good care
Had taken just seconds to strip wrappings bare.

I was left with returning some gifts to the stores,
And *all* of the cleanup of Christmastime chores.
It was now up to me to decide what to do
With leftover turkey and fruit salad, too.

While sitting there sulking in self-pity and gloom,
I saw my granddaughter skip into the room.

Her pixie face beamed as she climbed in my lap;
Her arms reached and circled my neck in a wrap.

"Oh, Grandma," she whispered, her eyes big and
    wide.
"It's the best Christmas *ever*!" My heart swelled
    with pride.
In one arm she cuddled her new teddy bear;
A bright Christmas ribbon was stuck in her hair.

She showed me the bracelet she'd made from a kit.
Shared her cookie with me—and we ate every bit.
My mood turned to gladness. Rejoicing, I smiled,
For now I saw Christmas through the eyes of a
    child.

—*Eleanor Christensen Parker*
Penn Yan, New York

Home for the Holidays

By Patricia Goodwin of Ottawa, Kansas

IT WAS Christmas Eve and Susan parted the curtains of her kitchen window to look down the lane for the umpteenth time. No vehicle in sight.

Disappointed, she turned and strolled through the big old farmhouse. Everything was ready and the entire family was gathered for her son Johnny's homecoming from overseas.

The house looked and smelled like Christmas—tree trimmed, cookies baked, holly and mistletoe hung over every doorway.

Earlier in the week, she'd sent her husband, Jim, out to get the biggest tree he could find. She smiled, recalling how he and his brothers struggled to maneuver it through the front door yesterday, their father shouting directions.

As always, Jim's parents, Nanna and PawPaw, were there. Christmas was the time of year they missed "the old place" most—and Susan didn't mind sharing the farm that had been part of Jim's family for four generations.

Heading back to the kitchen, she couldn't help parting the curtains again. "Don't worry, Mom, They'll be here soon," assured her son Mike, a high school senior.

"The Army won't let us down," chimed in her daughter. "They got him as far as Los Angeles yesterday."

"It's not the Army I'm worried about, Laura," Susan said.

Storm Warnings

"You mean the snowstorm? Awww, those weather forecasters never get it right. It passed *us* by so there's no reason to think things will be that bad in Chicago," Mike added.

Hearing their pickup truck outside, Susan grabbed her jacket and rushed onto the porch. But the look on Jim's face told her immediately that Johnny was not with him.

"What happened?"

"All flights out of Chicago are canceled 'til tomorrow. The airport's snowed in. Nothing landing, nothing taking off. I'm sorry, hon. I know you were really counting on Johnny being home tonight."

"But where *is* he?" Susan asked.

"I don't know. Couldn't get any detailed information. They said to go home and wait for his call."

"Oh, Jim, it's just not fair."

He pulled her close and let her cry until her sobs slowed. "Come on, let's go inside," he said. "It's time for dinner."

Susan took a deep breath. After all, she *did* have a house full of people she dearly loved.

After dinner and dishes, it was time for hot apple cider and their traditional stocking-hanging ceremony.

The older grandchildren had been busy earlier numbering small squares of paper and tossing them in a bowl. Nanna now held the bowl, mixing the folded squares with her fingers.

It was a tradition they'd followed for years. Everyone picked a number from the bowl, waited for it to be called, then chose a spot for their stocking on the mantel.

After the last one was hung, Nanna turned, "Now for our special stocking."

Tears filled Susan's eyes as she stepped forward with Johnny's stocking. Turning, she found Jim at her side with hammer and nail in hand.

"Pick your spot," he whispered, and together they tacked Johnny's stocking in place.

Stocking Stuffers

Within an hour, the Christmas story had been read, the children tucked in their beds, and their mothers busy with armfuls of packages until the living room was filled with gifts. Tomorrow morning was going to be fun—chaotic but fun.

"This old house has seen many a Christmas," Nanna reminisced. "Glad I'm still around to see one this big."

"I'm glad, too. I just wish Johnny could have made it," Susan sighed.

"Life can play unfair tricks on us no matter *what* we plan," Nanna noted briskly. "Let's fill those stockings."

She was a trooper. And right now,

that's what Susan needed. The two women spent the next hour filling all the stockings. By midnight everything was in place and everyone was asleep—except Susan.

Unable to drift off, she slipped out of bed and went downstairs. The aromas of the night's festivities lingered in the air.

She snuggled down in the rocker, tucking an afghan around her. Slowly, the serenity of the quiet room, lit only by tree lights, began to melt away some of her disappointment…

Susan stretched, not realizing she'd dozed off, and was startled to see the time. In just another hour she'd have to be up working on the turkey if Christmas dinner was to be on the table by noon! She hurried to the kitchen to put on the coffee.

Hearing a low rumble outside, she stepped to the window and caught her breath at the sight of a semi making its way down the lane.

Grabbing her coat, Susan slipped on Jim's boots at the back door and flew onto the porch.

The big rig was getting closer, black smoke puffing from silver pipes on either side of the cab. Finally, it ground to a halt and the passenger door blew open.

"Merry Christmas, Mom!"

"Johnny!" cried Susan, her face wreathed in a smile. "Welcome home!"

When 'Rubies' Grew on Moss

By Della A. Runka of Edmonton, Alberta

THE MOSS that grew in the cranberry bogs near our farm in northern Alberta was emerald green—and as soft and spongy as deep velvet. Sprinkled here and there over its surface lay the dark red cranberries so prized by farm wives at the time.

During the Great Depression, Mama didn't have the cash to buy cranberries for our homegrown Christmas turkey. But she was a gatherer, often scouting the land for treats for her family. She knew where to find wild blueberries, strawberries and raspberries—even the treasured cranberries.

I was about 5 years old when she took me along to the cranberry bog. I remember we walked across a small hay field, over a hilltop and there, ahead of us, the sun-jeweled blue waters of a little lake danced into view.

At the shoreline, Mama helped me into a tiny weathered wooden boat, seating me at the stern. In my hand I held tight to a little tin cup. Mama carried a syrup pail.

To my delight, we were soon skimming lightly across the water to the gentle splash of Mama's paddle. The sun sparkles stayed just ahead of us and out of reach, so I trailed my fingers in the cool water, trying to pinch the bubbles left by Mama's paddle.

Over the Water...

Golden birch trees lined the far shore of the little lake, and I can still remember how their leaves fluttered down, landed lightly on the water, then floated away like tiny yellow sailboats.

Following a small creek that linked that lake to another, we walked with difficulty in the bog, sinking up to our ankles in the springy green moss. But Mama had a special surprise for me hidden in her syrup pail.

She had split and hollowed out a small zucchini from her garden, making me a pretend boat that I could pull through the water on a long string as we walked.

When I tired of that, she showed me how to fill my tin cup with the glossy cranberries and empty it into her pail. The berries glowed like red jewels. I thought they were pretty enough to make a necklace!

Mama laughed and called them "rubies". (I'd never even *seen* a ruby, but I knew they must be very special.) She kept track of how many cups of the bright berries I had picked, praising and encouraging me until her pail was filled.

When we got home, she dried some of the cranberries and we strung them with fluffy white popcorn into long chains. Then we hung those garlands on our Christmas tree, and Mama said it was the prettiest one we'd ever had!

The rest of the cranberries she cooked with sugar and water to make the cranberry sauce that topped our Christmas turkey.

Sometimes we'd spoon that sauce over plain white cake and top it with rich farm cream for a delectable finish to our rather plain meals. Mama really knew how to make even simple food taste like a feast.

And Through the Years...

So many years have gone by since that day. Mama is gone, too. But she left me a ruby ring—a ring she never even wore. It was a little too big and, because she never felt she could afford to have it sized, it was tucked away in its tiny moss-green box. (I learned later that my father bought it at a secondhand store in downtown Edmonton because it was all he could afford.)

Sometimes I open that little box just to admire the ring. But the rubies nestled on green velvet remind me of Mama, and then I remember, in a rush, her love of nature, her thriftiness, her appreciation of simple things.

Most of all, I remember that day long ago, when we gathered the "rubies" that grew on moss...and all the Christmas love that we shared. ✻

Fragrant Wreaths Ring Out Montana Holiday Greetings

HIGH IN THE MOUNTAINS, Ann Knollenberg finds a Christmas kind of feeling…and the hardy, most fragrant boughs for her handcrafted evergreen wreaths, swags and centerpieces!

Finding beautiful boughs is a big part of Bitterroot Evergreens, the home-based business she owns with husband Dale. "The best-quality materials grow at just over 6,000 feet above sea level," confides Ann.

Since the valley they call home in Victor, Montana (nestled between the Bitterroot and Sapphire Mountains) is located at only 3,500 feet, they must head for the "high country" to gather their evergreens.

"I love going up to collect the first bunch of boughs. That first scent of Christmas is *so* wonderful," says Ann.

Working with the National Forest Service, the couple has a permit to harvest some 9,000 pounds of Grand Fir and (the most fragrant) Sub-Alpine Fir in an area that requires thinning. Last fall, they went every day for 3 weeks.

"We try to get our gathering done before the first heavy snow up there, and that means starting the beginning of October. We cut whole trees, but are limited to those 7 inches in diameter at chest height," Ann relates.

"We trim off the limbs to use in our wreaths, swags and centerpieces. The trunks are used for firewood. We don't waste a thing," she says with pride.

All their evergreen works of art are individually crafted by one of five employees, each with years of experience and a flair for decoration. "We trim them with pinecones, juniper berries, red bows and imagination," Ann says with a laugh. "We have so much fun, it really doesn't even seem like a job.

"Our Bitterroot Evergreen wreaths are fragrant and stay fresh for months if kept outside where it's cool. Some folks tell us that birds nest in the wreaths, so they have to leave them up all year long!"

Most of their business is as "made in Montana" as their wreaths, Ann says. "But we ship all over the country. And the majority of our customers are repeats," she adds.

While others are busy decking their halls with her fragrant boughs, Ann is busy filling orders—as many as 1,000 a year sometimes.

"The only down side to this business is that when we run low on greens, we can't get more because there's too much snow and it's too dangerous to go up again. I hate disappointing people, but they do order earlier the next year," she smiles.

Editor's Note: *To order Bitterroot wreaths, swags, centerpieces or loose boughs, call 1-406/961-3718, or visit www.evergreenwreath.com.* ❋

MOUNTAIN MAGIC and a sheer love of the Christmas season go into every rustic wreath, swag and centerpiece crafted by Ann and Dale Knollenberg of Bitterroot Evergreens.

THE FIRST NOEL comes to life each Christmas under the guiding hand of Sherry Blackston (top right). Together with family, friends and a merry menagerie, she delights in staging a live manger scene on her Ohio homestead. Visitors are welcome to celebrate the true reason for this magical season, and then get acquainted with Sherry's animals.

Living Nativity Brings Home True Meaning of Holy Night

SHEPHERDING livestock from one local church to the next during yet another holiday season, Sherry Blackston of Delaware, Ohio had an inspired idea. Why not host a Christmas pageant right in her own backyard?

"We had been lending out our animals to other Nativity scenes for years," she recalls. "I thought it would be a nice family project for us all to work together on and a good way to bring home the true meaning of the season."

"Home" for Sherry, her husband, Bruce, and their three grown children is the brick house her Irish ancestors built in the late 1860s, along with 35 acres of the original homestead.

Each December for the last 5 years, Sherry's family has pitched in to help her set up the stable backdrop (built by her brother), complete with manger and

star. They've also helped fill out her cast (along with neighbors and other relatives) as shepherds, magi, angels, Mary and Joseph.

"And each year," Sherry relates with delight, "someone has brought a real baby and placed it in the manger for at least a little while."

Sherry, who oversees the entire project—from supervising the costumes to choosing the carols for the CD player—limits her manger-scene menagerie to one Jersey calf, two donkeys, a ewe, pygmy goat and llama. But visitors are encouraged to stop by the barn and see the other animals, too.

"We have three llamas, a 1,000-pound pig named 'Wilbur', six sheep, two turkeys, five ducks, three pygmy goats, a horse, two donkeys, 50 chickens, five peacocks, 16 cats...and oh,

there are probably more," she chuckles.

The weekend before Christmas, dressed in a red Santa hat, Sherry passes out handwarmers to chilly actors, hot cocoa and candy canes to visitors and a focus on the real meaning of Christmas to the community.

Come rain, snow or starry night, the faithful flock to the tiny stable that's set up close to the country road that runs past Sherry's place. Sometimes as many as 100 visitors in one night will drive slowly by or stop to get a closer look.

"More people come every year," Sherry says, smiling. "One person tells a few others and they tell *their* friends... it kind of spreads by word of mouth."

Funny how good news and glad tidings often do.

Editor's Note: *The live Nativity is held the weekend before Christmas from 7-8 p.m. on Saturday and Sunday. Delaware, Ohio is about 20 miles north of Columbus. Follow State Route 315 out of Columbus, make a left on Hyatts Rd., then a right onto Liberty Rd. Go 2 miles to Ford Rd., then a mile to the site.* ❄

May the peace and blessings of this holy season linger with you and your loved ones the whole year through.

INDEX

Share Your Holiday Joy!

DO *YOU* celebrate Christmas in a special way? If so, we'd like to know! We're already gathering material for our next *Country Woman Christmas* book. And we need your help!

Do you have a nostalgic holiday-related story to share? Perhaps you have penned a Christmas poem…or a heartwarming fiction story?

Does your family carry on a favorite holiday tradition? Or do you deck your halls in some festive way? Maybe you know of a Christmas-loving country woman others might like to meet?

We're looking for *original* Christmas quilt patterns and craft projects, too, plus homemade Nativities, gingerbread houses, etc. Don't forget to include your best recipes for holiday-favorite main-dish meats, home-baked cookies, candies, breads, etc.!

Send your ideas and photos to "CW Christmas Book", 5925 Country Lane, Greendale WI 53129. (Enclose a self-addressed stamped envelope if you'd like materials returned.) ★